"What Do You Want?"
She Asked Him.

His expression was stern and his eyes were bright with a gleam she didn't quite like. "You know what I want, Pippa! I want you to come to Tsavo with me. I can't let you go back to Nairobi until I know why you hold back from me."

"I have work to do!"

He caught her by the shoulders, his fingers digging into her flesh. "I want you." The harshness of his voice made her shudder inwardly. "And what's more, you want me too. So it shouldn't be too difficult for you to arrange to spend some time with me."

ELIZABETH HUNTER
uses the world as her backdrop. She paints with broad and colorful strokes, yet she is meticulous in her eye for detail. Well known for her warm understanding of her characters, she is internationally beloved by her loyal and enthusiastic readers.

Dear Reader:

I'd like to take this opportunity to thank you for all your support and encouragement of Silhouette Romances.

Many of you write in regularly, telling us what you like best about Silhouette, which authors are your favorites. This is a tremendous help to us as we strive to publish the best contemporary romances possible.

All the romances from Silhouette Books are for you, so enjoy this book and the many stories to come.

Karen Solem
Editor-in-Chief
Silhouette Books

ELIZABETH HUNTER
Rain on the Wind

Silhouette *Romance*

Published by Silhouette Books New York

America's Publisher of Contemporary Romance

SILHOUETTE BOOKS, a Division of Simon & Schuster, Inc.
1230 Avenue of the Americas, New York, N.Y. 10020

ISBN: 0-671-57290-3

First Silhouette Books printing April, 1984

10 9 8 7 6 5 4 3 2 1

Map by Ray Lundgren

America's Publisher of Contemporary Romance

Printed in the U.S.A.

BC91

Books by Elizabeth Hunter

Silhouette Romance

With many fond memories of
Meryl Gourley Farrington

How often you and I
Had tired the sun with talking and sent him down the sky.
—Heraclitus: W.J. Cory

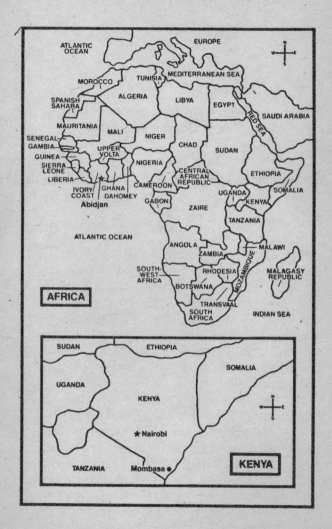

Chapter One

The camp was totally deserted now. Pippa Gregson slowed the Landrover and came to a stop
beside the place where her father had last pitched
his tent. It was a sad pilgrimage but one which
was necessary to her. It was here that she had last
seen him, shattered and broken by the actions of
her husband, Timothy, but still too proud to
accept anything from her by way of an explanation or an apology.

She had been foolish to offer him one, she
thought now. Timothy hadn't consulted her before he had published her father's findings as his
own. He had never consulted her about anything
that mattered all the days they had stayed together. She was a sadder, wiser woman now she was
without him, and, she hoped, a better person. If it
had happened now she would have known what
to do and would have exposed Timothy for the

fraud he was, but in those days she had been a young girl, baffled by what she had taken to be the love of her life and distraught at the threat of having her happiness taken away from her.

In the silence that followed the cutting out of the Landrover engine she could hear a light aircraft buzzing overhead and wondered who could be flying so far away from the recognised routes. This particular part of the Rift Valley was one of the most isolated parts of Kenya, which was what had made it so attractive to her father with his obsession for finding out more about our first ancestors, the relatives of the well-known Lucy, the earliest recognisable human-being ever to have been discovered.

The aeroplane buzzed overhead, flying dangerously low down the valley. The pilot waved a hand to her. She waved back without thinking. Perhaps it was someone she knew.

She walked across the valley to the gulley where her father had been found dead a few short weeks before and poked about in the soft soil at the foot of the cliff which showed so clearly the different stages of the making of the land. The Rift Valley had been formed by the same tumult that had seen the end of Sodom and Gomorrah, a vast crack in the earth's surface stretching through Asia Minor, halfway down the continent of Africa. Lucy and her friends had walked and talked and had their being long, long before the valley had been formed, but it had been this strange twisting of the earth's surface that had revealed so many finds, starting with Mary Leakey's in the Olduvai Valley in Northern Tanzania.

Pippa was so intent on her thoughts that she didn't notice that she was no longer alone until a deep masculine voice said angrily just behind her, "Did you tell anyone you were coming here?"

She turned quickly, her heart thumping, cross with herself because she couldn't rid herself of the instinctive fear she felt for all strangers nowadays.

"Who are you?" she demanded.

Then memory struck her with the force of a sledgehammer that she knew who this man was. She had met him only once before, a few weeks after her marriage to Timothy, and his strong, sunburned features had been burned into her consciousness for ever. She could remember it as if it had been yesterday: the contempt with which he had spoken to Timothy and the quite different way he had looked at her, stripping her naked in his mind as if that were the only meaning a female such as she could have for him. She had been more humiliated in that moment than at any time in all that had happened between her and Timothy. She knew now why that had been so. She had responded fiercely to that look in his eyes. She had wanted him every bit as much as she had known he had wanted her.

Joel Buchanan's recognition came more slowly, his amusement at her expense coming fast on its heels.

"Mrs. Gregson? What strange situations you do get yourself into. Didn't anyone tell you your father is dead?"

"A couple of days ago."

"You won't bring him back by coming here. I'm surprised your husband could spare you to make

such a sentimental visit, or is he hiding somewhere out of sight?"

Pippa forced herself to concentrate. "I haven't
seen him for two years. He went off to fight as a
mercenary down south and was killed shortly
after."

"Did you go with him?"

She shook her head. "We'd already parted
company."

Now what had induced her to tell him that? She
was very much in control of herself these days.
She dressed well, her whole life-style taking on a
sophistication her younger self would have gasped
at, not really approving at all, and she had
developed a technique of dealing with anyone
who came too close, especially those of the male
sex.

His eyebrows rose slightly, giving his face a
devilish look she remembered all too well.

"What brought that about?"

"Is that any of your business, Mr. Buchanan?"

"Is it?"

She was back in Nairobi, eating an ice-cream in
the café outside the Norfolk Hotel. It had really
been too cold and draughty a day to sit outside in
comfort, but she had been with Timothy, and that
was where he had chosen to take her so it never
would have occurred to her to complain. But it
was not Timothy she was remembering now, it
was Joel Buchanan and the way he had looked at
her, destroying her happiness in a single moment.

"Was that you flying around up there?" She
changed the subject. "You're a long way from
base."

"So are you," he countered.

"I had to come!" She shrugged her shoulders, holding her jacket closer about her. She jerked back her head, her mouth firming into a determined line. "I write books these days. I'm going to write my father's biography at the suggestion of some London publishers. I'll be able to set the record right at last."

She found herself thinking that Joel Buchanan's eyes were very grey, as grey as the sea round the English coast where she had stood so often these last two years, longing for the heat and the blues and browns of her native land. She shivered inwardly.

"You haven't said what you're doing here," she accused him.

He didn't answer for a long moment, then he said, "Have you time to climb up to the top of that cliff?"

"I suppose," she said reluctantly. Her shoes weren't suitable and it was a long time since she had undertaken such vigorous exercise. "If I'd wanted to go mountaineering I'd have come more suitably dressed—"

His smile was mocking, but not unkindly so. "I was only going to remind you of the sights and sounds of Africa you may have forgotten. Can't you smell the rain on the wind? If you stay here, you'll be bogged down in mud before you can say 'Jack Robinson.' I nearly had a fit when I saw you down here!"

"What were you doing up there?"

"There's a herd of elephants back there who've smelt the rain and are making for water. It's my job to see that nothing happens to them until I can get them safely into their usual park."

It was strange, but in all the times she had thought of him she had never wondered once what he did for a living. It was his physical presence that had overwhelmed her. He was over six feet, but looked larger, with a solidly packed frame topped off with the fairest hair she had ever seen on an adult. She had taken it for granted that he did something out of doors for the sun to have bleached his hair to that extraordinary colour, but what it was hadn't interested her at all.

"You're a warden at one of the national parks?" she mused aloud. "I never thought of that."

He shook his head. "I study elephants. That is, it's elephants at the moment. Unless we know their patterns of behaviour we won't be able to save any of the wild life. The human population of Kenya is expanding too fast not to want all the land in the end unless we can make it worth their while to share it with the game. Right now the government's in a listening mood because it's the animals that bring in the tourists, but the tourists don't have votes, and nor do the animals and that's what's going to count in the end."

"The tourist industry means jobs surely?"

"For the few. It's the farmers we have to convince if we want to keep our animals for future generations and I don't despair of doing that." He smiled slowly at her. "Not many farmers welcome a herd of elephants running over their land. They'll be moving through here in about an hour, so be a nice, kind girl and drive me back to my plane and then get going as fast as you can out of their way!"

"I've only just arrived!" she protested.

He stood a little away from her, his feet apart and his arms folded across his chest. She felt a stirring in her blood as she wondered what it would feel like to be caught up in those arms. She blinked, wrenching her thoughts back to the job she had come to do.

"You don't understand," she went on huskily. "It was here that Dad found that skull. I have to get the feel of the place if I'm going to write about it with any conviction."

Joel Buchanan said nothing at all. His eyes narrowed in the same appraising way they had once done in Nairobi, and then he turned away as if he had found her wanting, leaving her standing there, her fury whipping the hot colour into her cheeks.

"I'm not leaving!"

He turned back, laughter at the back of his grey eyes. "Of course you're leaving," he said. "It'd be fun to stand and fight until the elephants get here, but they're larger than we are and, whilst they know me well enough to avoid hurting me, they don't know you at all, and you'd be standing between them and the water they know is just over yonder."

"Can't you make them go some other way? They'll ruin this site if they walk all over it."

"What would you suggest I do?"

"You're keeping them away from the farm-lands, aren't you?"

"Right. I've spent the whole day pushing them towards this valley and there's no way I can turn them back now."

"Why not?"

The trumpeting that was coming steadily nearer answered for him. Joel braced himself, listening intently, his expression changing from one of amused interest to one of purpose and urgency.

"Get in the Landrover!" he ordered her.

She could hear the elephants more clearly now, shaking the dry trees as they came. She remembered being told as a child that elephants had a habit during the months of September and October of eating the roots of certain trees which made them exceptionally bad-tempered. She began to wonder if they were going to get out of the valley in time.

Pippa chose the passenger seat from instinct. It might have been her vehicle, but she was sure Joel knew the terrain and the complicated gears far better than she. Elephants, particularly African elephants, are huge animals, and drought-maddened elephants with the scent of water in their nostrils are every bit as dangerous as the very latest in military tanks, yet it was only when Joel had set the Landrover up a disused track to the top of the gulley that she began to realise the very real danger they were in. She gripped the canvas-covered seat as hard as she could to give herself some confidence.

"Cheer up, we'll make it." Joel's voice cut through her thoughts.

She turned her head sharply and studied his

profile for a long moment. Was he really as certain as he sounded? In Nairobi his confidence in himself had been so overpowering that it had completely sapped her own faith in herself, over-turning the basic assumptions on which she had based her whole life. It had been a few months before she had discovered that he had been right all along, but she had not forgiven him for being right. She doubted she'd ever forgive him for that.

The Landrover lurched dangerously and she was thrown against him. The contact made her flesh burn, lighting a fuse of excitement within her that was every bit as alarming as the approaching elephants. Her resentment that it should have been he who had found her at her father's site was like a bad taste in her mouth. For days after that meeting in Nairobi she had tried to exorcise him. Even Timothy had wondered what was the matter with her, she remembered with a shudder. Timo-thy's form of questioning had been violent and distressing. Because of it she had left him to live her own life, and the wounds to her self-esteem had slowly healed over. Now they were being rubbed raw again by the physical presence of the man beside her.

The elephants had reached the plane before them, leaving a tangled mass of metal in a heap in the middle of their path. Joel brought the Landro-ver to a screeching halt alongside and jumped out to take a closer look. Pippa joined him more slowly.

"What are you going to do now?" she asked him.

He went to the edge of the cliff they had just come up, looking down at the elephants through his field-glasses. Pippa shook some of the dust out of her clothes, ruefully thinking that it was the colour of dried blood. Then, instinctively, she turned just in time to catch a glimpse of the elephant close behind them, one huge beast that had separated itself from the rest of the herd as if seeking vengeance for their presence. She swallowed hard on the knot of fear in her throat.

"The leader of the pack is looking over your shoulder!" she breathed.

Joel's movements were as calm as hers were fevered. He moved out of the sheltering bushes, holding his hands wide.

"Hullo, old girl," he greeted the angry elephant. "It's only me! I'm ashamed of you for not noticing my smell all over that plane of mine. It was you who wrecked it, I suppose? I thought so!"

The elephant hesitated, snorting with fury. Slowly she reached forward her trunk, delicately sniffing the air ahead of her. Apparently she recognised Joel's smell and some of her anger left her. She trumpeted noisily in Pippa's direction, but Joel deliberately placed himself in front of her, masking her scent.

"Stand still," he said quietly. "She knows me—"

"*She?* I thought it a bull making all that noise!"

"The bulls don't travel with the herd. Those are all cows and their young down there. Let's hope this old matriarch goes back to them."

Pippa silently crossed her fingers. The elephant

took two steps forward, reaching her trunk over Joel's head to pick up Pippa's smell the better. Pippa froze, unable to move even if she had wanted to. She was sufficiently frightened to be able to taste her own fear on her tongue.

"Go on, my beauty," Joel said in the same calm tones. "Off you go and leave my girl-friend alone. She's with me. That's right, get a good smell of her and you'll know her when you meet again."

"She won't get the opportunity!" Pippa croaked.

"You never know your luck."

Slowly, the elephant lowered her trunk, shaking her head from side to side while she thought things over. She trumpeted one last time, backed away until she felt she could safely turn her back and then went cavorting down the track to join the rest of the herd down below.

Pippa sat down hard on the red earth, taking deep breaths to keep herself from fainting. It was the nearest she had ever come to dying and it was going to take her a little while to come to terms with the fact. She raised her knees, dropping her head down between them. She felt sick.

"Have a look now, Pippa," Joel invited her, handing her his field-glasses. "It's got to be one of the most fantastic scenes you'll ever see in your whole life!"

He thrust the binoculars into her hand. "Look down there, darling! Come on now, it's all over!"

She looked up at that, her eyes sparking with temper. "I'm not your darling!"

"Perhaps not yet," he agreed lightly. He pointed down below them to where the main body of the elephants were making their way through the narrow valley where her father had made the greatest find of his life, only to have it stolen by Timothy later on.

The rain would soon be with them, she thought dully. Already there was a green haze on the brush, a miracle she had witnessed several times before, a kind of last push of life in the dry sticks so that they would be able to make the best use of the water when it came. She had often wondered how plants could retain enough moisture, sometimes for years, to be able to green up when they sensed the approaching rain.

There were some fifty elephants lumbering along below them, one or two of them so small that they were having some difficulty in keeping up, and their mothers and young unmarried aunts were prodding them along with a gentle push from their trunks, making sure that none of them lagged behind. It was indeed a beautiful sight. Elephants really cared for one another, especially the females. They would prop up their elderly, giving them a crutch through the hardest parts, and they all took turns at keeping an eye on the youngsters. Pippa felt a great rush of affection for them. She had always had an admiration for the largest animal left on earth, and now that they were safely gathered in the valley down below she was no longer afraid of them but could observe their antics with the same enjoyment as did the man squatting down beside her.

He took the glasses from her and adjusted them for his own eyes, leaning his elbows on his knees as he watched the herd hurrying towards the rain that she could already see in the distance. It travelled towards them, a large black cloud, surrounded by sunshine, turning the golden grass to a dark shade of grey and leaving a bright green behind it.

"Where were you planning to spend the night?" Joel asked her.

"There's a mission beside Lake Turkana."

He shook his head, glancing at his watch. "We'll never make it. Have you any camping things with you?"

She had, but they had only been included as a last resort. She had no fancy to spend the night under canvas all by herself somewhere in Africa. She had courage, she thought, but the sounds of the African night were no longer as familiar as they had been before she had gone away to London to learn her trade.

"The nuns won't mind how late I arrive," she said with a confidence she was far from feeling.

"We might be able to rescue something from the plane. I'll just make sure the herd's headed in the right direction and then I'll go and look."

Pippa stood up with decision. "I want to leave now for the mission," she announced.

He stood up also, putting a friendly hand on her shoulder. "You don't have any choice, Pippa. If those elephants get headed the wrong way I'll be left with a hell of a lot of explaining to do. It's your fault I lost my plane, so it's only fair that you should lend me your Landrover." He smiled slowly, a wide, very masculine smile. "You may enjoy the company," he said.

She might; that was the trouble. She felt a

quiver of fear run up and down her spine. How ridiculous she was being, she told herself sternly. She was no longer a young girl with no knowledge of men or life; she was an experienced woman, a woman who had known both marriage and rejection—so why should she think it would all be quite different with this man? Joel Buchanan had looked at her once in Nairobi and he might as well have stripped her naked, but that had been two years before, and she was better able to handle herself now. If she didn't want to get involved with him, she wouldn't; it was as simple as that.

"I hired this Landrover on the understanding that only I would drive it," she said with a light shrug of the shoulders.

"I've no objection," he answered.

"I don't want to chase your beastly elephants halfway across Africa!"

"You don't know what you want, do you?" he retorted. "You never have had the courage of your convictions."

She could feel the hot blood staining her cheeks and hated him for it. This whole mess was of his creating and there wasn't the least reason in the world why she should make it easy for him. She climbed into the Landrover and automatically reached for her bag, searching inside it for her lipstick and the jewelled flapjack which had been a present from one of her admirers in London. She snapped it open, making a face at herself in the glass as she liberally applied colour to her lips and a dusting of powder to her face. She always had a honey-coloured tinge to her skin to go with her dark-brown, beautifully shaped eyes and her short curly hair, and the sun of the last two days had tanned her to the colour of toast, making her powder several shades too pale. She might have done better to have left it off, but it was too late now. At least she felt better with it on.

Joel got in beside her, his eyes unreadable as he watched her. She could feel her heart thumping like a drum as she waited for his comment, but it never came.

"Well?" she prompted him.

"I preferred the girl I met in Nairobi, in a home-made dress, sitting on the edge of her chair and looking as if no man had ever desired her before. She had her husband sitting beside her, but she was a real person, not just a glossy exterior."

"I was very much in love with Timothy," she claimed, nettled.

His eyebrows shot up in a look of sceptical enquiry. "You thought you were," he said dryly.

"I was!"

He pointed lazily along the trail which went along the top of the escarpment. "Drive on, my sweet! We can have this argument any time in the next few days; my elephants aren't going to hang around for anyone."

She was on the point of doing as he ordered her out of habit. Like many weak men, Timothy had had an image of himself as a macho individual who had only to bark a command for any woman to obey him, and all the time she had been with him she had gone along with that because it was easier than quarrelling with him. But she was no longer married to Timothy and she didn't owe this man anything at all. She set her mouth in a stubborn line and went on with the task of making up her face. . . .

She never saw him move. She felt a small prick of warning in her flesh and that was all. Her bag was taken from her and flung onto the rear seat and she, herself, was lifted clear out of the driving seat and set down hard on his lap, his arm holding her against him like a band of steel.

His lips took hers with a violence that made her gasp. For an instant she tried to win free, pushing with both hands against the hard wall of his chest, but to no avail. His tongue forced its way between her lips, finding hers with a seductive mastery. Some of the tension went out of her body and she moulded herself against him, revelling in the feel and taste of him. She had never much enjoyed Timothy's attempt at lovemaking, but Joel had lighted a spark the first time she had seen him, and he was now busily fanning that ember into a raging fire. He had found the vulnerable place between her shirt and trousers, and his hand travelled up her bare back, trailing his fingers along the line of her spine and finding the softer swell of her breasts and her rapidly hardening nipples.

An instant later she was alone in the passenger seat and he was walking round the Landrover and climbing into the driving seat she had so recently vacated. He turned the ignition key and the engine roared into life, compounding the thunder of her blood in her ears. Pippa swallowed hard, striving to regain her control over herself.

"I hate you!" she said, her voice hard and cold.

"At least now you look like a real person again, not just a painted doll."

"Is that why you kissed me?"

He slanted a glance sideways at her and she looked away hastily before those steely grey eyes should see any of the secrets she wanted to keep from him. She didn't want him knowing too much about her. It had taken her a long time to become the person she now was, and she wasn't going to be pushed back into the mess she had been in when Timothy and she had finally parted company. No one was ever going to be allowed close enough to her real self to be able to do that to her ever again. No one. She had promised herself that over and over again in the last two years.

"I kissed you because I wanted to—and because you wanted me to." He set the Landrover in motion, making his way towards his ruined aeroplane. "Have you got a check-list of the equipment you brought with you?"

"It's in the pocket of the door beside you." She sniffed, humiliated by the ease with which he could turn his attention onto such mundane matters when she was still quivering with the desire his touch had roused in her.

He took it out, keeping one hand on the wheel, apparently finding no difficulty in keeping the Landrover on the track and looking down the list at the same time.

"With the stuff I've got in the plane we ought to be able to manage," he said cheerfully.

She sniffed again. She stared out at the greening grass, withdrawing herself from his presence by pretending that he wasn't there at all. She wouldn't even look round when he drew up again at the mangled remains of his plane.

He jumped out, extraordinarily light on his feet for such a large man.

"Cheer up, sweetheart," he bade her, running a finger down her short, straight nose, "I'll be too busy chasing my elephants to be chasing you for the next few days, more's the pity!"

"Then you can start by keeping your hands to yourself!" she snapped.

"If that's what my lady really wants," he said, before he turned to pull everything he could out of the wrecked plane. He tossed everything he thought they might need into an unruly pile beside the Landrover whistling as he worked.

He was decidedly the most exasperating man she had ever met.

Chapter Two

Pippa was aching from head to foot. She had fleeting dreams of a hot bath and the time to wash the red dust out of her hair and her clothes, but still they drove on, following the elephants at a safe distance, going wherever they went, sometimes fast and sometimes more slowly. It gradually became clear to her that Joel was pushing them inexorably in the direction he wanted them to go, towards the nearest national park and safety from the poachers who were ever busy where the prospect of ivory was concerned.

When the rain caught up with them there was no time to put up the top of the Landrover, and it wouldn't have done them much good if they had, for it was full of holes where it had been worn away by rubbing against itself.

"This is the most unpleasant drive I ever remember!" she burst out as the water dripped down the back of her neck.

Joel wasn't even listening. "They'll stop for the night soon—at the next water-hole probably—"

"Where we can camp beside them in the rain, I suppose?"

"There's a Turkana village not far away."

"Isn't there somewhere civilised where we can stay the night?"

"Tomorrow night maybe. You'll have to settle for a mud hut or sleeping under canvas tonight." His lips twitched. "Never mind, I'll be with you," he added maliciously.

She stirred restively in her seat. "It isn't funny, Joel," she said at last. "I don't know what you thought that time in Nairobi, but it didn't mean anything and it was a very long time ago. I've grown up since then. I have plans for my life and they don't include sexual adventurers like yourself!"

He slowed the Landrover to a stop, swivelling round to take a good look at her. The rain had stuck his lashes together, accentuating the deep grey of his eyes. His hair had flattened and darkened, taking on a reddish tinge from the surrounding mud. If she looked anything like him she didn't want to know, she thought. She looked down at her beautifully tailored safari suit that was now clinging to her legs in a sodden, crumpled compress. She probably looked worse than he did—women always did, with their hair straightened by the weight of the driving rain and their faces washed clean of any pretence of make-up.

"Timothy noticed, I suppose?" he said gently.

Everyone had noticed! Pippa had had none of the social weapons at her disposal to hide her feelings in those days. One moment she had been sitting beside her husband, eating her ice-cream and listening to his grumbles about something or another, and the next moment Joel had been standing beside her, grabbing her whole attention to himself.

"Aren't you Joe Walker's daughter?" he had asked her.

"She's my wife. Pippa Gregson. Mrs. Timothy Gregson," Timothy had interposed.

Joel had shown no sign of noticing the interruption. "Perhaps you'll have lunch with me," he had gone on. "I'm staying here at the Norfolk, but we can go somewhere else if you prefer?"

"I—I couldn't," she had said.

"Why not?"

She had felt the force of his personality right down in her toes. She had wanted to go with him so badly that she had almost cried with frustration at having to refuse him.

"I'm with my husband!"

Joel's eyes had flickered briefly over Timothy and away again. "It's your father I want to talk to you about, not your husband."

"Oh?" She hadn't known what to answer to that. She had felt guilty every time her father's name was mentioned—she still did, come to that, but then she had started like a fawn, catching her lower lip between her teeth and flushing like a fool.

"Pippa—" Timothy had started to say.

"I wasn't talking to you," Joel had cut him off. "Are you coming, Pippa?"

"I can't!"

He had held out a hand to her and she had started to rise, forgetting all about Timothy. Joel's fingers had tightened over hers, drawing her to her feet. He had looked at her and she had been acutely conscious of every detail of her own body, more conscious than she had been on her wedding night or at any time since with Timothy. Her mouth had twisted into a wry smile as she thought of that night and the nights that had followed. She had been bitterly aware that this man was not Timothy.

She would have gone anywhere with Joel and all three of them had known it. She would remember till she died the wicked amusement in his eyes as he had said, "Come to lunch and dinner, Pippa."

"She'll do nothing of the kind!" Timothy had answered for her angrily.

"Well, Pippa?"

His hand had released hers, but only to pull her more firmly against him, his fingers brushing against her breast as he tried to lead her away. It had been that that had awakened her to some sense of reality.

"I can't!" she exclaimed.

Joel's face had looked suddenly bleak. "Aren't you going to do anything about your father?" he had asked her angrily.

"I'm Timothy's wife," she had tried to explain.

"What's that got to do with it?"

"I don't *know* that Timothy didn't find the bone."

He had let her go with an impatience that had left her bereft and shaking. "Your father feels your desertion very badly," he had said.

She had tried to explain it to him. "Timothy was there," she had told him. "Timothy says exactly how it happened in his book. Have you read his book?"

"I know your father," was all he said, and he turned on his heel and walked away.

Timothy had never forgiven her for her reaction to Joel Buchanan. Fortunately Timothy had never known that she had met Joel again in the Norfolk Hotel and that the only reason she hadn't given in to him was that her father had interrupted their *tête-à-tête*. Her father had been as delighted to see her as if she hadn't taken Timothy's side in the quarrel. Indeed, he had never mentioned Timothy or his own work once, though he had expressed concern that she was looking so thin and pale.

"Married life doesn't seem to agree with you," he had grunted, and Joel had lifted his brows and had added, "Are you surprised?"

The rain ceased as suddenly as it had started.

"Timothy is dead," Pippa said, annoyed with herself because she couldn't quite stop the tremble in her voice, "so it hardly matters whether he noticed or not. I wasn't a particularly good wife to him, but I always tried to be loyal to him. I

wouldn't really have allowed anything to happen
between us, you know."

"You might not have been able to prevent it."

She would have found a way somehow! She
shut her eyes against the dazzle of the newly
arrived sun sparkling on the numerous puddles all
about them. Timothy had carried on as if she had
betrayed him as it was. What he would have done
to her if she had even kissed Joel she preferred
not to think about. Timothy was dead and she
didn't think she owed his ghost much considera-
tion. She was free to do as she liked, but not with
Joel. She was afraid of Joel, afraid of the effect he
had on her, and afraid most of all of his finding
out that she wanted him as badly now as she had
then.

"You're too conceited to be true," she said with
a smile, tilting her hat over her eyes to hide them
from him. "I was very young then and easily
pleased. I'm more choosy these days."

"I'm glad to hear it!"

She tried to shut out of her mind the knowledge
that Joel hadn't been alone in despising Timothy.
Sometimes she had thought her father had held
Timothy's being his son-in-law in greater contempt than he had Timothy's theft of his discov-
ery.

"If we go much further we'll run out of petrol,"
she remarked, "and then you'll have to follow
your elephants on foot!"

A muscle moved in his cheek. "You sound as if
you'd like that. What would you do? Hang
around the Turkana village until I got back?"

The Turkana were a nomadic and warlike people who had little time for strangers. Pippa had never known any, but she had heard stories about them since childhood. She had always heard that a Turkana had only two purposes in life: more land and more livestock. As she had neither, she didn't fancy her chances of receiving much hospitality at their hands.

"I'll thumb a lift back to Nairobi."

He laughed. "You're more sure of yourself than you were, but I don't think I can allow you to do that. Better the devil you know—"

"I don't know you!" she denied.

"You will."

The elephants settled for a newly formed water-hole, rampaging through the water and squirting each other like children at play. It was a beautiful sight to see the gigantic grey animals rolling over and over and trumpeting with delight after the long drought they had suffered. Each of the babies was tenderly washed and cared for and then escorted back to dry land where it was covered with a coating of dust to keep down the irritation of insects. Pippa began to wish that she could join them. Her clothes had dried on her and were as hard as a board with the mud that clung to them and her.

Joel watched them with a proprietory air. He pointed out each of the cows, telling Pippa the name he had given her and her history in the herd.

"That's the one you have to watch," he said eagerly, leaning forward in his seat as he pointed out the largest of them all. "She's the matriarch, the one they all follow. If you can get her to go where you want her to, the rest'll follow. I call her the Empress."

Pippa laughed. She thought she had a strong look of Queen Victoria, though it couldn't possibly have had anything to do with her size, for Queen Victoria had been a wee bit of a woman and her namesake must have weighed several tons. It was more to do with her air of consequence and the dignity with which the massive cow rolled happily over and over in the mud.

They waited until the whole herd had bathed and drunk their fill of the collected rainwater. Only when they had all settled down to pulling up the fresh, succulent scrub, cramming great branches of the trees into their mouths, Joel decided they could be safely left for the night.

"I hope those sleeping-bags are drier than they look," he remarked as they set off across the grassy open space towards the edge of Lake Turkana, once known as Rudolph. This was the jade sea of legend, which few white men have seen even today except by air. Yet it had been familiar to Pippa all her life, for it was here that her father had come across the fossil of a primeval elephant and had started his search for evidence that early man had also inhabited this desolate land when it had been wet and well watered and the living had been easier than it was now.

One-and-a-half million years old Joe Walker had reckoned the elephant to be, and now they had proved that mankind was older than that.

After finding the elephant he had found a skull of *Australopithicus africanus*, but it had been the later skull of *Homo erectus* that had caused all the excitement. Joe Walker had told his wife and daughter that he would be a famous man from then on, but he had reckoned without his son-in-law. Timothy and Pippa had been staying at her parents' camp, and they had been due to leave the following morning. Timothy had woken Pippa in the middle of the night and had told her they were leaving early. He had left her behind in Nairobi while he had gone on to London, taking the skull with him and claiming it as his own find. Pippa's mother had hardly spoken to her daughter after that, but Pippa as Timothy's wife felt that she had to take his side, even though nobody else had.

"What else do you do besides nanny elephants round the countryside?" she asked suddenly.

"Do I have to do anything else?"

"I just wondered where it was going to lead?"

"I enjoy what I do," Joel told her. "What else would you have me do? Make a name for myself by sucking up to the television producers of the Western World?"

"There are worse things," she said defensively. "Knowledge is only worth anything when it's shared with the rest of mankind. My father was always saying that man would manage the present much better if they could understand their own beginnings better."

"Since when did you listen to your father?"

She flushed. "I'm writing his biography. I don't see what more I can do to put his views across."

Joel put out a hand and squeezed her knee by way of an apology. "Okay, that was below the belt and not entirely deserved. How did you ever get mixed up with someone like Timothy in the first place?"

"I fell in love with him," she said.

She wished he wouldn't touch her. She thought she was going to be able to manage if he didn't touch her, but every contact with him brought a tidal wave of response that threatened to drown any common sense and the hard-won shell of independence she had gained for herself in London.

They came upon the Turkana village suddenly, without any warning. One moment there was nothing but Africa ahead of them, and the next she could make out the temporary huts, most of them no more than roughly constructed shelters for both men and animals, rising up out of the background of the never-ending thorn trees and scrub. She might not have been able to pick it out as soon as she did if it had not been for the sudden greening of the land, leaving the golden sheaves of grass that formed the walls and roofs standing out more noticeably than they would have before the rain had passed overhead.

Pippa was not surprised that the village was expecting them. She had long ago learned that everyone knew everyone else's business in Africa, just as it was impossible to be alone. There were always eyes watching, ears listening and silent footsteps coming and going. Sometimes they were men and sometimes animals, but anyone who could read the signs would know exactly

what was going on anywhere in their own territory.

The headman was seated outside the home of
some of his wives, some ostrich feathers in his
headdress betokening that he had killed a man in
his time and was entitled to call himself a warrior.
He wore a single robe, but his array of weapons
was formidable. Round his feet were his spear
and his clubs, and he wore razor-sharp wrist and
finger knives and a selection of long, thin needles
on which he would skewer any intended victim.
Pippa shivered at the sight of him, glad that she
had Joel with her. She tried to imagine how she
would have felt if it had been Timothy beside her
and failed dismally. Timothy would not have been
here and that was that.

Joel pushed her half behind him and took a step
forward, greeting the old man in his own language. At once indignant, Pippa allowed her
anger to subside gently. That was another difference, she reflected. If Timothy had been with her,
it would have been she who would have been
bargaining with the headman and for that Timothy would have reaped nothing but contempt.

It was only after they had been invited to seat
themselves on the ground that Pippa realised that
however warlike the Turkana might be, they
laughed more than any other people she had
come across. They chaffed Joel good-naturedly
about his elephants, his whole way of life, and
then for being unable to travel without taking his
woman with him.

"Enjoy yourself with your find from the bush!"
they teased him as they escorted him to a recently

erected structure where the headman had said
they could spend the night. "This woman is no
stranger to our land, is she?"

"Her father was Joe Walker."

"Ay-ee, the lover of old bones. How many
elephants did you have to pay for his daughter?"

Joel laughed with them. Pippa put a suitably
modest expression on her face and pretended she
couldn't understand what they were saying. She
didn't want to be known as Joel's woman—even
less did she look forward to spending a night
alone with him in this makeshift shelter. She
turned her back on the whole proceeding, preferring to watch the large group of women who had
appeared from nowhere to stand and stare at the
newcomers. They were dressed in little more than
loin-cloths and hundreds of heavy necklaces,
some of them made from tiny coloured beads
strung on wire, and others from the potent black
seed known as *enus,* while still others came from
the root *ekeriau* which would keep the wearer
safe from both man and beast.

One of the headman's wives doubled up with
giggles when she saw that Pippa was looking at
her. She approached her shyly, poking at her
white skin with bony fingers, and then, with great
daring, she took off her own plain metal circle
that denoted her married state and placed it
round Pippa's neck.

"But I'm not married!" Pippa protested.

A silence fell over the group. Pippa tried to
remove the circlet but her fingers couldn't work
the catch. The next thing she knew, Joel grasped
her by the arm and almost threw her inside their

makeshift accommodation. The crowd roared
with laughter, applauding Joel's action. Pippa
knew they were laughing at her, not with her, and
her indignation knew no bounds.

She was angrier still when Joel joined her in the
low-roofed shack.

"How dare you lay a hand on me?" she said to
him.

He stood in the entrance, looking at her. Then,
very slowly, he spread out his hand, revealing a
small portion of the *ekeriau* root which he put in
his mouth, chewing it hard before spitting it out
again on the floor at her feet.

"Do you have to show off in front of a bunch of
savages like that?" she demanded. "Aren't you
man enough to live by your own rules, instead of
descending to theirs?"

"The rules between a man and a woman are the
same everywhere," he answered.

Yes, but they didn't chew roots to gain extra
potency where she came from! She opened her
mouth to tell him so, but thought better of it.
There was no point in admitting that she had
understood the threat behind his chewing on the
root. It was better by far to pretend that she
thought him mad.

"Most men pretend to some kind of gallantry
where women are concerned," she agreed. "If
you had a spark of humanity in you, you'd have
driven me to the mission as I asked you to!"

He squatted down beside her, his hair outra-
geously fair in the shadowed hut. She would have
liked to have pushed it back from his face, and,
once the idea had occurred to her, her fingers

burned with the desire to touch and run their way
through that luxuriant growth. He had no right to
have such soft, springy hair, nor to have such
long, mysterious lashes, and as for his mouth, she
couldn't wrench her glance away from the slanting, determined smile that was coming closer and
closer to her own parted lips.

"I wanted to have you with me," he said.

"Too bad! All I want is a bath and a good
night's sleep, undisturbed by anyone."

She could see his tongue between his lips, and a
spark of excitement made her flesh prickle with
anticipation.

"That isn't all you want," he contradicted her.

"It would do for starters!"

He laughed softly. "There isn't much water in a
Turkana encampment. You'd probably have to
walk a few miles and carry it home yourself."

"It'd be worth it! I feel a mess as I am."

She felt surrounded by him as he put a hand on
the floor on either side of her hips, leaning
forward onto them.

"You look infinitely more desirable now than
you did when you hadn't a hair out of place and
all your emotions in the deep-freeze—"

"Rubbish!" she murmured.

She began to search for some means of escaping him, before she succumbed to the heady
masculinity of his challenge, for it was a challenge, even she could recognise that. He had
known that she had forgotten everything that
mattered to her when she had first seen him
standing there in Nairobi, and he meant to re-

mind her of the power he had over her, but she wasn't going to play that game with any man! Timothy's whole idea of marriage had been one of rights and duties, the rights being his and the duties being hers. She shivered inwardly with remembered disgust. Never again! *Never, ever again.*

Joel caught her change of mood and a frown appeared between his deep-grey eyes.

"What's the matter, sweetheart?"

"I can't bear to have you touch me!"

He stood up with a single, lithe movement that set her heart beating a powerful and quite different message from that of her memories.

"I'll see what I can do about that water you wanted," he said.

He pulled the blankets aside at the entrance to the hut, revealing the spear that some wag had plunged into the ground, a signal as full of meaning to all these nomads as a "Do Not Disturb" notice on a hotel bedroom door. It meant that a woman was entertaining the owner of the spear and, as Joel had no spear of his own, they had supplied one for him.

Joel turned and looked at her over his shoulder, the spear in his hand. Beyond him the sun was setting and the whole western sky had changed to a mixture of coppery gold splashed with blood red. Almost, Pippa wanted to call him back to her. She knelt up, her whole body poised and eager for the confrontation.

"Did you want something?" he asked her, his tone dry.

She shook her head. "No, nothing."

And he went out the door.

The night was like black velvet around her, full of the chatter of insects singing their endless song, reminding her of the teeming life that was going on all about her. She wanted to be a part of that life. She wanted to lie down close to Joel and feel his body against hers, not to be separated from him by the whole width of the stamped-down earthen floor. She wriggled farther into her sleeping-bag, giving up the idea of sleep for the time being.

She never heard him move, had no inkling he was even awake until she felt his fingers against her face.

"Can't you sleep?" he asked her.

She hardly dared to breathe. "No."

His arms scooped her up off the floor and carried her across the hut to where she had carefully laid out his bedding, as far away from hers as was possible.

"You'll sleep now," he said quietly.

"What makes you think so?" she retorted.

"Because all you need is a little loving." He put her gently down, climbing back into his own sleeping-bag. "A lot of loving," he amended, pulling her firmly into the circle of his arms.

She screwed her eyes tight shut, fighting the temptation to say nothing at all, to do nothing but just to let it happen to her.

"I don't want to make love with you," she said at last, her voice a mere whisper of sound. But she did want to, that was the whole trouble, she did and she couldn't understand herself for wanting it. It was as if she'd never been rejected by Timothy at all.

Joel blew gently on her closed eyes and kissed her even more softly on the lips. "Go to sleep, Pippa, and don't worry so. I can wait until you can't wait any longer, and I don't think I'll have to wait very long."

She could hear the rumble of laughter in his chest below her head, but she didn't move. She was comfortable for the first time that day, uncaring of what he thought of her, and it was in just such a vulnerable mood that she drifted off into sleep and dreamed of the smell of rain and the blood-red sky of the setting sun.

Chapter Three

She awoke with that suddenness that is so much a part of living in the bush. For an instant she thought it was some kind of a noise that had awakened her, but then she realised it was the arrival of the sun, which the roof of the shelter had been unable to shield from her eyes. She blinked at the dappled effect, easing her shoulder blades into a more comfortable position. She had slept better than she had expected, and, whatever its dangers, she was looking forward to the coming day with a relish that hadn't previously had a part in her life.

Outside the shelter a wood fire was burning. The scent of it assaulted her nostrils, making her sneeze and, for a moment, she was afraid she'd woken Joel. It was only then that she realised that part of her sense of well-being was that she'd been using his shoulder as a pillow. She explored the edge of her sleeping-bag with tentative fingers, belatedly realising that the two bags had been zipped together and that her lower limbs were inextricably entwined with Joel's.

She made a small movement, easing herself away from him and he stirred in his sleep, flinging a heavy arm across her. Pippa felt the breath knocked out of her and stayed as still as a mouse while she thought about what to do next. How had he come to zip their bags together anyway? He had no right to do such a thing, certainly not while she slept through the whole proceeding! How could she have done such a thing?

She moved her head a fraction of an inch so that she could look her fill on his sleeping face. It was a strong face, darkened by the sun, and made to seem darker still by his ridiculously fair hair. Even in sleep his mouth was closed in a firm line and his jaw gave nothing away. She wouldn't think of Timothy asleep just then, she promised herself, because comparisons were odious anyway and she was almost sure that her erstwhile husband wouldn't come out of the comparison well, and that depressed her. There must have been a time when she had been in love with Timothy or she wouldn't have married him. It all went to show how very dangerous being close to a man could be. She probably would end up being just as disillusioned with Joel if he stayed around long enough.

She moved again until she was able to see him more clearly, searching for some fault in the long, male body beside her, something to justify all her suspicions of him. All she felt was a desire for him to wake up and notice her.

As if in answer to her thoughts, he moved his arm more closely about her, pulling her back against him and muttering something under his breath she couldn't quite hear. She collapsed in a heap beside him, relieved to have the decision taken out of her hands. It was incongruous enough that she wanted this man to make love to her as she had never wanted Timothy. If she allowed Joel to possess her body, perhaps she would find it as disappointing as ever. It would be the best way of getting him out of her system once and for all.

His hand found the vulnerable space between her shirt and trousers and slipped up to find the curve of her breast.

"Sleep well?" he said against her ear.

Her intake of breath hit the back of her throat, making no sound at all. She rubbed her foot against his leg, turning her face away from him.

"You look far more like the girl I remembered from Nairobi when you're asleep," he went on, his laughter more like a growl in her ear. "This is nice, isn't it? It makes all the rest worthwhile."

"To whom?" she demanded sharply. "Not to me!"

He leaned up on one elbow. She could feel the weight and the warmth of his body against hers. She made to push him away but, as her hand found the nakedness of his chest, she couldn't resist the temptation of moving her fingers against him.

He dropped his mouth onto hers, brushing her

lips against the harshness of his beard before tempting her with his tongue. A wave of excitement passed through her, making her muscles quiver with anticipation. She knew at once that he had felt her response by the subtle change of expression on his face.

"Why deny it, Pippa? You want me as much as I want you, don't you?"

He eased her more firmly beneath him, undoing the buttons of her shirt as he did so. Pippa held her breath until a buzzing in her head made her release it again. She did want him! That was the trouble, because she couldn't understand her own reactions to him. She concentrated on trying to remember how she had felt on her wedding night when she had thought she was in love with Timothy—and he with her. It had all been her fault, he had told her. She was cold, frigid and unloving. A man wanted something more in his arms than a frightened, hysterical girl. Not that she could remember being in the least bit hysterical—only humiliated and disillusioned that this was all she could expect from her married life, whoever's fault it had been.

Joel's voice became more urgent. "You do want it, don't you?"

"Yes!"

She made one last effort to conjure up Timothy's image in her mind, but he was dead and gone and only Joel was there with her, the wood smoke in their nostrils and the smell of Africa surrounding them on every side. It was Joel's lips on hers, Joel's hands caressing her flesh and Joel who was filling her mind as he would soon take her body. She arched against him, her own hands no less busy in exploring the wood-hard muscles of his back and neck. It was too late to turn back now, she thought, and she wondered that she felt no regret in the inevitability of their coming together.

She closed her eyes against the pride she felt in the pounding of his heart against hers, only to find herself left abruptly alone, Joel rising to his feet without giving a thought to his nakedness, a superbly masculine silhouette outlined against the rays of the morning sun.

"What's wrong?" she complained. The anticlimax of it all made her want to cry. Had he, too, been disappointed, finding her as cold and unloving as Timothy had claimed her to be?

"Take a look!" he suggested wryly.

She heard the running hooves tramping over the floor and smelt the flock of goats long before she saw them. She began to laugh because it was better than crying, pulling the sleeping-bag close up against her to hide her nakedness.

"Get out of here!" Joel commanded the goats, pulling on his trousers. They paid him no attention at all. They were everywhere. One of them was taking a bite out of the roof, another doing her best to pull the shaky shelter down around their ears.

Pippa sat up, still laughing. "Their timing is impeccable!" she gasped out. "D'you think their owner is trying to tell us it's time we got up?"

"More likely his idea of a joke!" Joel stormed. "Wait till I get my hands on him. I'll wring his neck for him!"

Pippa sobered, her eyes enormous. "I think I'm grateful to him," she said abruptly.

"*Grateful* to him! Pippa—"

She lay down flat on her back, refusing to look at him anymore. It was easier to deny her need for him when she couldn't see him, or the outraged way he was looking at her.

"I will be grateful to him later on," she amended. "Just now I don't seem to feel anything very much."

She missed the softening of his expression. "I wish I could say the same," he retorted, his voice dry. "You'd better get up if you want some breakfast before we get after those elephants. I'll be outside when you're ready."

Pippa put off the moment of getting up for as long as she dared after Joel had gone. She relaxed all her muscles, one by one, breathing deeply as she did so, until she felt better and could almost face the thought of sitting beside Joel all day in the Landrover with something like equanimity. She was a fool, she told herself, to allow any man to affect the careful restraints she had placed on her emotions these last years. Did she want to put her happiness in hostage to a man again? She was worse than a fool, she was stark, staring mad!

When she finally pulled herself out of the sleeping-bag, the goats had gone and, in their place, someone had put a wooden hand-carved vessel filled with water. Pippa separated the two sleeping-bags, rolling them up ready for stowing away in the Landrover. When she was satisfied with their appearance, she went over to examine the water, only to find some fronds of greenery lying on the surface, making it difficult to see if it was clean or not. She knew this to be an old trick to stop the water from spilling when it was carried long distances on some young girl's head. She thought, as she had thought so often in the past, how unfair life was to the female sex. If it had ever fallen to the men to walk miles every day for a jar of water, there would be piped water the whole world over by now.

Pippa washed her hands and face. She was beginning to feel better. She could even think of Joel without her innards turning to water. It all went to show that she had been right in thinking it was nothing more than a severe case of propinquity. As soon as she was on her own again she would never give Joel another thought. Of course, that hadn't been quite how it worked out last time, but then she had had Timothy to remind her of him night and day, until the contrast between the two men had been like a body-blow every time he had brought up Joel's name.

There was no sign of Joel outside, and she told herself she was glad. The Turkana women giggled when they saw her, unable to believe the whiteness of her skin and the funny clothes she wore. One of them poked her in the ribs, calling her attention to some freshly caught fish they were cooking over the fire. They made gestures to tell her that it had been caught that very morning and that she was to eat as much as she wanted, for that day there was plenty for everyone.

It tasted good. Pippa hadn't realised she was hungry until she tasted the roasted fish on her

tongue. As a child she had frequently gone fishing
in the river with her father and had watched him
cook the catch over an open fire afterwards. No
other fish had ever tasted half as good as those
ones had, though these came pretty close. She
smiled at the women and tried to tell them so,
laughing almost as much as they did at her
faltering attempts to find the few words of Turkana she had persuaded her father's manservant
to teach her.

When she'd finished eating, she began to wish
that Joel would come back and rescue her from
the attentions of her female admirers. What had
at first been rather fun was beginning to strain her
good nature until she was hard put to it not to
brush their questing fingers out of her hair and
thought that if another sharp nail tried to scrape
the white off her skin she would have hysterics.
She tried to distract the giggling women by asking
them where the elephants had gone, but elephants were an everyday event in their lives,
Pippa was not.

"I must find Joel!" she insisted, backing away
from them, shaking her head at them when they
came running after her.

She took refuge in the back of the Landrover,
slamming the door shut behind her.

"My word," Joel greeted her, "your female
friends seem as determined to get you out of your
clothes as any of your men friends!"

"Speak for yourself!" she said crossly.
"Timothy—" She broke off, unwilling to finish
that particular sentence.

"Timothy liked you better with your clothes on, I suppose." Joel finished it for her. "I can't say I'm surprised—"

"Timothy was my husband!"

"What's that got to do with it? He wasn't your lover and you'll never be free of him until you admit as much to yourself."

The hot blood flooded into Pippa's face. "You know nothing about it! Of course Timothy loved me!"

Joel merely looked amused. "My dear girl, Timothy never loved any woman. You'll have to look elsewhere for a man who'll appreciate all you have to offer."

"Well, I shan't be looking in your direction!"

His smile was quizzical. "No?"

"No! And don't patronise me, Joel Buchanan. I've learned how to manage by myself very well since Timothy left. You forget I'm a widow, not a young, inexperienced girl, eager to hang on your every word!"

Joel opened the door and leaped lightly down onto the ground. "I forget nothing. You'd do well to remember that sometimes." His tone lightened as he smiled at her over his shoulder. "I've been around elephants far too long not to have taken on at least one of their characteristics." He threw the keys of the Landrover in onto her knee. "Drive round to the shelter, my sweet, and I'll pass our things out to you. I'm right in thinking you don't want to do your own packing?"

"Quite right," she agreed with a shudder. She had enough of being poked and patted for the time being. She kept telling herself that what she

wanted was to be alone, but she didn't really. She
was too keyed up by the thought of spending
another day in Joel's company. It would probably
turn out as badly as her other experiences with
him but she didn't care. There was just the chance
that everything would go right for a change and
then nothing would tear her away.

She crouched in the back of the zebra-striped
Landrover to receive their two bundles of bedding and the few other things they had taken into
their borrowed makeshift shelter.

"Don't tell me," Joel said when it was all
stowed away, "you expect me to drive you to the
mission now and hurry up about it?"

She clambered over the back, seating herself in
the passenger-seat, dangling the keys on one
finger, her smile provocative.

"I expect to chase elephants all day. Isn't that
what you're going to do?"

"I can't promise to get you to the mission
tonight either," he warned her.

"It doesn't matter. I can't think my credit
stands very high with them just now anyway."

He raised his eyebrows in mute enquiry.

Pippa jerked the keys towards him. "Don't
flatter yourself that they won't know where and
with whom I spent last night. News travels fast in
this part of the world."

"They won't think any the worse of you for
taking shelter for the night."

Pippa had no such faith in their charitable
instincts, or was it that she wasn't really averse to
being linked with Joel no matter on what terms?

Joel went back into the shelter one last time,

leaving Pippa to brood on her own. The trouble
with her, she told herself roundly, was that she'd
never been quite sane where Joel was concerned.
She had no idea what he was really like, or
whether she liked him or not. All that she knew
was that he raised her blood-pressure to fever
pitch every time she saw him. And who should
know better than she that that sort of thing never
lasted? There must have been a time when she
had loved Timothy, though she could barely
remember what she had felt at the time of their
wedding. Whatever feelings she had had for him
had wilted and passed away in the face of his
constant complaints and accusations that she was
both frigid and unloving on the rare occasions
when he had held her in his arms.

It would probably be the same with Joel. She
had no reason to think otherwise. If she wanted to
get him out of her system for good and all, the
best thing she could do was stick with him like a
limpet until the fires he lit inside her merely by
glancing in her direction turned to the ashes of
disillusion, as she was sure they must. If she got
hurt in the process, at least no one else would
ever know. Timothy had managed to hurt her far
more than Joel ever could because he had de-
stroyed all her dreams. At least Joel couldn't do
that to her. A widow such as she would be a fool
indeed to indulge in the sort of dreams she had
had, if only because such dreams and real life had
never had anything to do with one another.

Joel got in the Landrover beside her, banging
on the door with his open hand. Pippa jerked
herself upright, her attention caught by his action.

He grinned at her over his shoulder. "That's better," he applauded. "I don't like it when you go all broody about the past. He wasn't worth it, you know. He knew that, even if you didn't."

"He always said everything was my fault."

"Well, he would, wouldn't he?" Joel went on cheerfully. He put a hand over hers, and she was very conscious of the contrast between this man's hand and any other that had ever touched her.

"He could have been right," she said.

Joel turned and faced her. "What was your fault?" he asked her slowly. "Come on, tell me, Pippa! What was your fault?"

Pippa was very conscious of the Turkana pressing closer all around them. She couldn't, she simply couldn't, discuss the intimate details of her marriage with Joel now! She very much doubted there would ever be a time when she would want to, but now? How could he expect it of her?

"I prefer to leave it in the past where it belongs," she said stubbornly.

"If you can." He put out a hand and patted the side of her face in a movement so exquisitely gentle that it brought tears to her eyes. The back of her throat felt as hard as a lump of wood and was beginning to hurt as she blinked away the tears.

Smiling, he pinched the end of her nose. "One day I'll tell you about my first impression of you. It won't be when we have a crowd looking on though, because you still blush like a young girl even if you are an old married woman! Now, I'd better go and say our goodbyes."

"Should I come too?" she offered, hoping he

would veto her having to get out of the Landrover
again.

"No, you stay where you are!" His smile grew
again slowly, creasing the firm flesh of his cheeks.
"I'll tell them how grateful you were for their
hospitality, and I for the loan of the spear that
kept all the other hopeful gentlemen away from
you!"

She was saved from having to make any comment in reply because he was already gone by the
time she had mustered her resources to put him in
his place. Timothy had never teased her, nor she
him. She wasn't sure that she liked the thought of
being a constant source of amusement to Joel, but
she had to admit it was better than the silent,
tight-lipped criticism that was all she had ever had
from Timothy.

It soon became clear from the sounds of laughter all about the Landrover that Joel was enjoying
himself as the centre of attention of the Turkana
warriors. Pippa wondered where he had learned
to speak their language, for few Europeans would
have attempted the task, preferring to stick to the
lingua franca of the whole of East Africa, Swahili.
All Pippa knew about the Turkana language was
that it was so sophisticated that it had twenty-
three verbs alone to describe a person's walk. Yet
Joel seemed to have no difficulty in making himself understood, cracking jokes and sometimes
pointing in her direction so that she could guess
whom he had picked on to be the butt of his
humour. She stretched her feet out in front of her
and wiggled her toes, pretending not to notice,
and she had almost persuaded herself that she

didn't mind what he thought of her when he jumped into the driving-seat beside her, still laughing.

"I'm glad you find me so funny!" she burst out.

He slanted a glance at her. "You speak Turkana?"

She shook her head. "No."

"Even so you ought to know better. No African male would ever discuss his woman with another man. Women aren't important enough—"

"Is that so?"

"Maybe they're too important. Shall we go?"

The Landrover shot forward, taking her unawares, so that she had to hang onto the roof-support for dear life to keep her seat. She turned and looked behind them, clenching her teeth to keep them from rattling.

"They're running after us!" she told him.

He slowed the Landrover to allow the young men to catch up with them, calling out some comment to them. The men waved their spears, forming an escort all around the vehicle as they ran, their long-drawn-out howl of *"hu hu hu"* accompanying every step they took. After a mile, the first one tired and fell back, followed by another, and another, until there was no one left, only a few tall, stately figures standing in the dust, waving their spears above their heads.

Pippa threw back her head and laughed. "What a thing is fashion! Even the Turkana have taken up jogging for their morning work-out!"

Joel took his hand off the wheel and rested it briefly on her knee. The shock of the contact travelled up her leg with the speed of lightning, reigniting the desire she had felt for him that morning. She sat further back in her seat, eyeing his hand as if it were a snake about to strike at her. She took a deep breath and then another and felt a little better.

"I can still take you to the mission," Joel said.

She scarcely heard what he said. "Do you ever go jogging?" she asked him.

"I would if I ever had to sit behind a desk all day for a living. Why? Should I?"

"No! I mean, no, you're in very good condition—"

"How about you?"

She was surprised that he should ask. "Me? I prefer swimming. Timothy didn't swim."

"Hence the preference?"

She was shocked by the idea. "Of course not!" But she wasn't nearly as sure as she pretended to be.

They reached the elephants just as they were starting out on their day's rush towards the coming rains. Joel went right round the herd until they reached an outcrop of grey rock that stood a few feet above the water-hole where the elephants had spent the night.

"Coming?" he asked her.

She was nervous at getting out in such an exposed space. Who knew what animal might have been lurking in one of the scrubby trees that had found a space to grow between the smooth, weathered rocks.

"What are you going to do?" she asked him.

"I want to check them over before the Empress

decides which way she's going to take them today. Yesterday's rain has practically disappeared already, and she'll be nervous of not finding any water before nightfall."

It seemed to Pippa that the Empress was very much in control of the situation. The huge cow waved her trunk from side to side, her head raised as if she were looking for something. A couple of adolescents attended her, moving backwards and forwards between her and the rest of the herd. Another cow, one of her tusks split by some hunting expedition from the past, trumpeted a warning and the Empress turned towards the outcrop of rocks where the two humans were standing, flapping her ears back and forth to make herself look even bigger than she was. Then, recognising Joel's scent, she let blast a trumpet of sound and walked slowly back to the main body of the herd. A few seconds later, she was prodding the latest baby to the side of the herd for Joel to see, its anxious mother running along behind, her trunk hovering protectively over her young.

"It'll never keep up!" Pippa exclaimed.

"They'll slow down to the pace of the youngest and the most infirm, but the old lady is worried they won't find water before nightfall. It's a pity we can't give the youngster a lift, but I somehow don't think its mother would understand."

Pippa had never seen such a young elephant before. It barely came up to its parent's knee as it stumbled over the rough ground. It must have been very newly born indeed, for, even as they moved along the edge of the herd, its legs were already firming and it was soon trotting along quite well.

"They'll be off in a moment," Joel said with satisfaction. "We'd better get ready to follow them."

And move off the herd slowly did, pushing the babies and the elderly into the centre of the herd to prevent them from falling behind, making their way towards the well-watered lands of the south where it had already been raining for several days. The clouds moved slowly in the opposite direction, many of them to be burned away by the sun over the semi-desert of the arid north.

"What do you think of my elephants?" Joel asked with a grin.

"I'm getting to like them," Pippa said.

"And me?"

She licked her lips, not looking at him. "I could get to like you too," she admitted, "I think."

"You're not sure?"

"No, I'm not sure," she said.

Chapter Four

Ahead of where they were travelling they could look out across a hundred miles of country stretching into the distance, most of it burned dry by the long drought, and only here and there greened up by the approaching rain. In the sky the black clouds scudded back and forth, occasionally dropping their rain in a moving pillar that swirled across the plains.

"Hang on to your seat," Joel warned Pippa. "I'm going to cut them off from going through that village over there. With any luck we can get them to go round the *shambas* and make for the Samburu. They came from the game reserve there in the first place, until they ate out the whole area, helped by the rains failing for three years running. If I can get them safely back there, they should be all right for this year at least."

Pippa enjoyed the chase, once she had mastered the art of riding the Landrover much as one would a bucking horse. She could well understand the appeal the elephants had for Joel. She was caught up in their journey herself and wanted nothing more than to see it to a successful conclusion. She was still surprised at how fast the great beasts could travel, despite the handicap of a new-born baby. It was all the more remarkable when she considered the sheer bulk of food each elephant had to get through in a day just to keep going.

When they had successfully moved the herd over to one side and into a recently rained-on valley, complete with water-hole, for the night, Joel slowed down for the first time in what seemed like hours.

"We'll need what petrol we have with us for tomorrow," he began apologetically. "I'd like to drive you to a village for the night, but—"

"It doesn't matter. I could sleep sitting up!"

"Tired?" He smiled as she rubbed the small of her back. "You'll be aching lower down in a minute. I'll pitch a tent for the two of us later on and light a fire. Think you can cook us up a meal?"

Pippa thought she could. She hadn't much experience of living out of doors, but anyone could open a couple of tins and heat up the contents over a fire. She was hungry enough to eat practically anything, for it was a long time since she had eaten her breakfast of freshly cooked fish that morning.

Joel avoided the yellow-fever trees closest to the water, choosing instead a flat-topped acacia tree on higher ground. Pippa sat on her haunches and watched him pitch the tent, trying to make it look bigger and less fragile by sheer will-power. Surely, he didn't expect the two of them to share that?

"Keep the flaps closed when you're not going in and out," he instructed her. "There's some mosquito netting over the main entrance, but insects will get in anywhere if they've a mind to. That's one of the drawbacks of the rainy season."

Pippa made a face at him. "I've left my anti-malaria tablets behind. I didn't think I'd need them so far north."

Joel sighed, saying nothing. Instead, he put all his energies into cutting a neat hole in the ground outside the tent, in which he laid and lit a small wood-fire, putting his whole being into blowing on the burning grass until the punk sticks caught and then the hard wood that he'd gathered up from round about.

"Isn't the fire supposed to be my job?" Pippa queried, not moving a muscle.

"Right. Feel like getting us some more firewood?"

Pippa looked nervously about her. She didn't like to tell him she was afraid to go far by herself. She knew something of the habits of wild animals, but not enough to be able to tell their tracks apart, or to know where to look for the danger signs of an approaching large cat, or a snake, or some other horror that might attack her.

"Are you coming too?" she asked.

He gave her a long, level look. "I wouldn't let you go two feet if you were in any danger."

He fed the fire from the pile of dead wood he had already collected and then went over to the Landrover to collect their bedding and cooking things. Pippa knew she ought to help him, but she was afraid. She threaded her fingers together, astonished by the amount of dirt that clung to them. When she looked down at herself she saw she was covered with a fine red dust from the day-long chase after the elephants. There was nothing romantic about dust, she thought. Joel had probably forgotten all about those intimate moments they had shared that morning. She wished she could forget as easily. Even when she wasn't looking at him, she could see the way he had looked when the goats had interrupted them, his naked body lean and hard, and the way his muscles had moved, and how much she had wanted to touch and be touched by him.

He threw the cooking things down at her feet, standing, his feet a little apart, over her like a giant.

"Are you going to cook us something to eat?"

She nodded, not trusting herself to speak. She looked through the tins and chose some corned beef and baked beans, putting them to one side.

"Will that be enough for you?" she said at last. "I could make some sort of bread on the baking sheet. Will that be all right?"

"Do as you like," he said tersely.

Her fingers shook as she tried to open the tin of corned beef with the key provided. Out of the corner of her eye she watched Joel standing there, not moving a muscle as he watched her efforts.

"Was Timothy unkind to you?"

She was startled and the key slipped dangerously, cutting into her forefinger. She sucked at it, her eyes filling with tears.

"No."

Joel squatted down beside her, took the tin out of her hands and finished opening it himself. He eased the meat out into the pan she held out to him and rootled around in the bag, looking for the tin opener for the baked beans. When he found it, he opened the beans with a flick of his wrist and added them to the meat.

"You'll find some gourds filled with fresh water in the Landrover," he told her. "I could do with a cup of tea, couldn't you?"

She saw with relief that the Turkana had been generous with their supplies of water. There was more than enough for tea and the bread she wanted to make, as well as for their breakfast the next morning. She reached in for the nearest of the gourds and pulled it towards her. These strange fruits made excellent containers for carrying water or anything else, some of them holding up to a gallon inside their tough, dried shells. They had another advantage in that they weighed practically nothing in themselves and so could be carried quite easily.

Coming back to their camp, she paused to look down towards the water-hole. The elephants were still stamping around in the muddy edges of the water, but it was the wart hogs which caught her attention, coming to the water in their family groups, their thin, tufted tails held high as they trotted back and forth. Soon other animals would approach, taking their turn in the queue to quench their thirst. Nervous antelope, their hides twitching with anticipation, would move forward, followed by the wildebeests and the zebras that were nearly always seen in each other's company. For once they would be ignored by the predators that hunted them for food in their common interest in finding enough water to see them through another day.

It was one of the most beautiful evenings that Pippa ever remembered. The yellow trunks of the fever trees stood out starkly in the evening sun, their leaves rustling gently in the breeze that had sprung up in the last half hour. There were giraffe to be seen now too, picking at the flat tops of the acacia trees as they made their stately way towards the water. Behind them came a pride of lions, the cubs keeping a wary eye on their mother as she nudged them forward into the evil-smelling mud that edged the rapidly diminishing pool.

It was only when Pippa was pouring out the water into a kettle that she realised that she hadn't been at all afraid as she had watched the animals, any more than they had paid attention to her. It was the time of truce, when all animals were safe from one another. Except human beings. They played by their own rules and broke them just as easily—as Timothy had. She would do well to remember that in her dealings with Joel.

The bread—or *damper* as the Australians

would have called it—turned out rather well. Pippa felt proud of her efforts, and there was a lilt in her voice as she called Joel to come and eat.

"We can sit on that dead tree and watch the animals while we eat," she suggested, banging on the wood with an empty saucepan to get rid of any unwelcome lodgers in the silvery, brittle fallen tree.

"As long as we eat up quickly," Joel agreed. "The insects will arrive with the darkness and we'll be eaten alive."

Such a fate seemed hard to believe, however, as they sat companionably side by side and tucked into their food with all the hunger of a day spent in the open.

"It's been fun, hasn't it?" Pippa said suddenly, scraping her plate clean with a small piece of bread.

"It isn't over yet," Joel reminded her.

"What else do you do besides chasing elephants round the country?" she asked him.

"I specialise in studying the ecology as a whole. Conservation has always been a big thing in Kenya. You could say it started here, first of all with the national parks and, more lately, with the setting up of the tree people, who've spread all over the world, researching the damage that's being done by cutting down the remaining rain forests of the world. These people are also trying to determine what will happen if we don't replace the forests."

"What will happen?"

"The atmosphere will change, turning the

whole planet into a desert. The Sahara was once forest land and look at it now! It's the trees that keep up the oxygen levels which we all breathe. If they go, we go; it's as simple as that."

"It sounds a grim prospect," Pippa commented.

"It needs thinking about," Joel rejoined. "We have to live with the rest of creation, not apart from it."

Pippa poured them both out a mug of tea and sat back, blowing on the boiling liquid to cool it.

"It's a long time since I spent a night outside like this. When I was a child, we often went on safari with nothing more than a tent and a few supplies. My father believed that everyone ought to spend time every year away from the softening influences of city life—"

"But Timothy didn't agree with him?"

"He wasn't at his best when he didn't have everything on hand. I can't imagine him as a soldier. I didn't believe he meant it at first when he said he was going south to fight. I thought it was just an excuse to get away from me, until I heard he'd been killed and all his personal things were sent back to me. It was rather horrible."

Joel took a sip of his tea. "Forget him."

"But he must have hated it all so, slogging through the bush with a heavy pack on his back—"

"Where did he die?"

"In Angola."

"Then he probably travelled around in a helicopter. Forget him, Pippa. He's nothing to do with you any longer."

She wished it were true. "I was married to him."

Joel slid along the tree-trunk towards her, lifting her chin to force her to look at him.

"Not all marriages are made in heaven," he mocked her. "You had remarkably little in common with him."

"How d'you know? He had his faults, but he was always faithful to me. He had a very high ideal of marriage—"

"Like stealing from his father-in-law? There isn't much to being virtuous if you've never known temptation. The only thing I can't understand is why you should ever have thought Timothy to be the man for you."

"He . . . I . . ." Pippa almost gave up trying to explain the impossible. "I was flattered—I think. He talked to me at first, *really* talked to me. I don't remember that anyone else ever did. My parents were always much too busy and there wasn't anyone else."

Joel put down his cup, placing a hand on either side of her face, puckering her mouth with his thumbs.

"When I saw you in Nairobi, I didn't want to talk to you. I don't now. How d'you feel about me?"

She put a hand over his and withdrew it again, as if the touch of his skin had burned her.

"I don't know," she admitted.

"You knew this morning," he pointed out.

"No," she denied at once. "I wasn't thinking this morning."

"Are you thinking now?"

She was unable to restrain the quiver of excitement that shot through her. "I'm used to doing my thinking alone," she said.

He lowered his mouth to hers, taking possession of her lips with a harshness that made her wonder if somehow she had made him angry. She felt shattered by the contact, and her mouth opened in protest, only to be filled by his exploring tongue. She put both hands against his chest to push him away, but her muscles refused to obey her, and she found herself clinging to the rough material of his shirt as if she wanted to tear it off him.

She felt rather than heard the rumble of laughter in his chest and gave up the task of escaping his embrace, throwing her arms around his neck and pulling him still closer to the soft, responsive curves of her body. The words "I love you" stuck fast in her throat, shocking her into a realisation of what was happening to her. She wrenched herself free of his restraining arms and stood up, her knees shaking so badly that she almost sat down again more quickly still.

"The insects are beginning to bite," she complained.

"It's as good an excuse as any," he acknowledged.

Pippa licked her dry lips. "I have to be careful, not having my anti-malaria tablets with me," she babbled on. "I remember my father having malaria once. He was terribly ill with it. For weeks he went round with a funny yellow colour to his skin and a singing in his ears. We were always afraid that he might get it again."

"The cure in those days did turn one yellow."
Joel took up his cue. "The singing in his ears
could have been the quinine he was taking."

Pippa shrugged. "I'm not going to take any
risks, all the same!"

"Very wise," Joel said dryly. "In which case
you'd better turn in and get behind that mosquito
netting. I'll take a walk while you're getting
yourself ready for the night."

Pippa resented his going, glossing over the fact
that she also would have resented his staying. She
couldn't recognise herself in this mood. All she
knew was that she didn't like herself very much at
that moment. There was nothing new in that,
however. She had spent years now disliking herself and what Timothy had made of her.

She washed up the tin plates and mugs they had
used for their supper, drying them on the cloth
she found amongst the other cooking things. She
didn't really want to go to bed yet. Only a few
minutes before, it had been daylight and now it
was completely dark, there being no twilight so
near to the Equator. Good heavens, it was only
just seven o'clock and, whilst she had led a quiet
life recently, she hadn't yet taken to going to bed
with the birds.

Joel had put a hurricane-lamp beside the tent.
It would have been kinder of him if he had taken
the time to light it for her before going off, she
thought. The matches beside the lamp were damp
with the evening dew and refused to spark, adding to her troubles and the burden of what she felt
for Joel. After a while, she gave up the attempt
and felt around in the darkness for the opening to

the tent. The stars were like huge diamonds in the sky above her, and the evening chorus had come out to do its bit to add to the noisy backdrop of Africa. Usually she liked to listen to the noises of the night, but now it only added to her irritation. The howling laughter of a hyena was almost the last straw. To keep the animals away she should have built up the fire before she'd left it. If it went out before Joel got back, he would probably blow his top at her lack of forethought, and she would be the last to blame him.

Inside the tent, she fell headlong over one of the bedrolls and swore softly in the darkness. Where was Joel? It was ridiculous to worry about her modesty when it was pitch dark and she couldn't see her hand in front of her face. Besides, he'd already seen more of her than any other man had except Timothy. Timothy again! She wished she could forget all about him, but it seemed to her that whenever she shut her eyes, there he was, petulant and disapproving, just as he had been in real life. If only he hadn't left her this legacy of guilt she might be able to make something of her life. As it was, every time Joel came close to her, she felt as if she were betraying Timothy and herself too. Timothy had hated Joel, and Pippa knew why. Timothy hadn't wanted her himself, but he hadn't wanted Joel to have her. He had seen at once that Pippa had been knocked sideways by the attraction she had felt for Joel in Nairobi, and he had never ceased to remind her that she was his wife, his property, and he was never going to let her go. "Timothy's dead and

I'm free," she said out loud. "I can do as I like and it's nobody's business but my own."

She was asleep when the rain came pouring down. She turned over, surprised to see Joel leaning over the lit hurricane-lamp as he adjusted its flickering flame.

"Have you been back long?" she asked him.

"Long enough," he grunted. "I hope your tears were because you missed me?"

"I was asleep," she said defensively.

"It was some dream you were having. If you hadn't woken of your own accord, I'd have offered you a cup of tea in a few minutes."

"You mean I was crying in my sleep?"

His face was shadowed and mysterious in the flickering light and his hair shone in reflection to the flame. Pippa's heart jumped at the sight and she hastily averted her eyes away from him. The rain was making a pattering noise on the canvas, adding to the intimate atmosphere inside the tent. She reached up her hand and accidentally touched the canvas above her.

"Don't do that!" Joel commanded her, too late because the damage was already done and a steady drip began to drop down onto her bedding. "Don't you know enough never to touch wet canvas?" he roared at her.

"I'm sorry."

He lifted her bodily, sleeping-bag and all, and laid her down beside his own bag. He took a small medicine bottle out of his pocket and shook a tablet out onto the flat of his palm, reaching out of the door for the two mugs of half-cold tea he had left there before coming inside.

"It's more rain-water than tea," he apologised, handing the tablet to Pippa. "Get this down you and then go back to sleep!"

Pippa picked the tablet off his palm. "What is it?"

"There were a couple of mosquitoes whining around in here when I came in. It's better to be sure than sorry." He shook himself out a tablet and swallowed it down quickly. "I'd have given it to you before if I'd known you were going to flake out at this hour."

"I couldn't light the lamp," Pippa said defensively. "The matches were wet. What time is it?"

"About half-past-nine."

Her eyes widened. She had slept for longer than she had thought.

"Will it rain all night now?"

"Could be. We'll be all right in here. We're on high ground and we shouldn't be disturbed, although the fire went out long ago."

"I forgot to make it up," Pippa confessed.

"The rain would have put it out anyway." He glanced at her worried expression and made a gesture with his mug for her to finish her tea. "I cooked this up in the Landrover with one of the tablets of fuel I kept in the plane. We can manage without the fire."

Pippa chewed on her lower lip. "I'm not much good at this kind of thing, am I?"

He reached across and took her mug from her, his fingers touching hers. The contact sent a tingle up her arm and she swallowed hard.

"You don't seem to be doing too badly," he said. "A little practice and I'd take you anywhere."

She flushed with pleasure. "Really?"

He laughed under his breath, dropping both mugs on the far side of his sleeping-bag.

"Yes, really, my love," he mocked her gently.

He leaned over her, putting a hand on either side of her slender body. "One goodnight kiss and then I'm turning out the light. It's been a long day and you need your beauty sleep—"

He kissed her with a passion that brought a rush of blood to her head. She didn't need malaria to have a singing in the ears, she thought, as she felt her bruised lips with her finger tips. She was about to say as much when she realised that he was already wrapped up in his sleeping-bag, his head turned away from her, fast asleep.

Chapter Five

It stopped raining sometime before dawn. When Pippa woke up and crawled out of her sleeping-bag to face the day, the sun was just rising above the horizon, causing the dampness to rise in clouds of mist that reached almost to the tops of the trees. Pippa shivered in the unexpected coolness of the morning and pulled on a sweater over her now rust-red, dusty trousers and shirt. In the distance she could hear a lioness hunting, the distinctive cough of warning sounding out through the quiet of the early morning.

She slipped out of the tent with only a brief backward glance at the still sleeping Joel. She was glad to spend a little time alone, because she had to make up her mind about the best way to handle her relationship with Joel. He knew her as Timothy's widow, as he had once known her as Timothy's wife, but she didn't feel like either when she was in Joel's company. She felt like a young girl on the brink of her first love affair. Worse still, she was very much afraid she was in love with Joel, and she still had no idea what it was that he wanted from her. It could be a brief affair, or something more long term, but she didn't think it was marriage that he had in mind. All he wanted was to ease the itch of desire he felt for her—but would she be content with that?

"Good morning."

She turned so quickly that she almost lost her balance. Joel still bore the marks of sleep on his face, but she thought she had never seen him looking more handsome. His shirt was open to his waist, revealing the smooth skin of his chest, covered with a light dusting of the same blond hairs that grew on his head. When he took a deep breath her attention was drawn to the flatness of his stomach and the way his trousers moulded the strong muscles of his legs. By contrast, she felt a weakness in her own body that was as exciting as it was inconvenient.

"Good morning," she responded breathlessly.

"What got you up so early?" he asked her.

She looked across the misty scene and poked at the damp remains of the fire from the night before.

"I thought I'd try to find some dry wood and light the fire."

"Very brave! Aren't you afraid of meeting that lion that's hunting out there?"

"I wasn't going far from the camp," she assured him. "I thought, if I kept to the high ground, I might see the kill." Her voice took on a note of excitement. "Could we, Joel? She can't be far away!"

"What makes you think it's a she?"

Pippa was glad to show off her knowledge of the ways of lions. "It's almost always the female who does the hunting. Sometimes they hunt in pairs. Lions are lazy animals, and none more so than the male of the species. Yet he always gets to eat first, before his wives, and before the cubs are allowed so much as a taste of the meat. It doesn't seem a very fair arrangement."

"In a drought, the cubs might not survive anyway. The mature lions have to make sure they have the strength to mate and produce new life that will survive in better times. That way the species has a better chance of maintaining its numbers in the long run."

Pippa shook her head. "It doesn't seem very noble in the tradition of the King of the Animals to me."

Joel tucked his still open shirt into his trousers. "Compared to the other cats, the lion is a gentleman. No leopard will warn her prey that she's hunting."

"What about the cheetah?"

"The cheetah is too shy to survive in the modern world. Their enemy is man. They won't hunt if they think they have an audience. They'd rather stay under cover and starve to death."

"Can't the tourists be kept away from them?"

"Not if they're spotted. To get photos of cheetahs is a highlight for most people on safari. The rarer the animal, the more a sighting is prized."

"So nothing can be done?"

"Not a lot. At the moment we're stopping the tours from going into certain areas in the parks where we know the cheetahs are breeding. Sometimes it works and sometimes it doesn't."

Pippa bent over the remnants of their fire, poking the burnt pieces with a handy stick. She was rewarded by a small curl of smoke and blew hopefully on the grey embers. At last a small flame burst into life, and she excitedly dropped a small bit of dry wood into the hole with a triumphant cheer.

"Well done," said Joel.

"Well done? It's brilliant!" she retorted. "Don't just stand there, Joel Buchanan! Fetch some water and I'll make us a cup of tea!"

"We'll make a woodsman of you yet!" He smiled at her.

Fetching the water, he filled the kettle for her. She looked up briefly as he handed it to her and, for a moment, he and she were the only two realities in the whole world. She stared at him, her eyes seeing only the slight shadow of his beard on his cheeks and the tilt of humour in his mouth. She didn't know how it happened, but one moment she was kneeling on the damp ground and the next she was wrapped in his arms, straining upwards for his kiss.

The heat of his body warmed her through and through. Her hands found the opening of his shirt and rubbed against his chest. The feel of him was precious to her, and she was reluctant to let him go when he gathered her more firmly against him, his lips bruising hers in the harshness of his kiss.

A minute later, she felt herself being lowered to the ground, his whole weight on top of her.

"Pippa?"

His eyes were black with emotion and she could feel an answering thunder of need in her blood.

She felt betrayed when he groaned and rolled away from her and she lay on her back on the damp ground, blinking back the tears that threatened to overwhelm her. He didn't want her! He had been tempted for a moment, but when it had come to it he had put her on one side. It had to be her fault, because she hadn't made a single move to stop him and yet she had still failed to give him what another woman would have known by instinct how to give.

"What's the matter?" she asked him, hunching her shoulders against his reply.

"The time of day, I guess," he ground out. "When I do make love to you, I prefer it won't be in a pool of mud."

Pippa lay very still. "Are you going to make love to me?"

He pulled himself to his feet, brushing down his clothes with a careless hand.

"You'd better believe it. You've kept me waiting longer than I like to think about, but sooner or later—"

She shivered with something very like excitement and sniffed. She was feeling better already.

"I'll make the tea," she said.

"Do that! And you'd better change your clothes while you're about it. You look more like a hippopotamus than the woman of my dreams!"

"Thanks very much!"

But when she stood up, she thought he had a point. Her already dust-stained clothes were now streaked with mud and water and stuck to her uncomfortably as she moved to the far side of the fire, as far away from Joel as she could get.

He watched her with his head on one side and she noticed his eyes were still black and that his fists were clenched into two balls as though he were afraid of what he might do if he relaxed. Was that because of her? The thought brought a tingle of pleasure to her. Perhaps she wasn't such a hopeless failure after all.

There was no sign of Joel when she re-emerged from the tent wearing clean, though rather crumpled, khaki stretch-jeans and a green T-shirt of a heavier knit than the one she had been wearing before. Pippa searched the terrain with her eyes, looking for him. She could see the grey shapes of the elephants, squirting each other with water down at the pool. There was something up in one of the fever trees, she noticed, and went to the Landrover to borrow Joel's binoculars to see what it was. When she had them trained in on the tree, her heart jumped within her as she saw it was a leopard. What was it doing about, at this time of the day? She had always thought leopards were nocturnal animals. Had it been hunger that had drawn this one down to the water pool when it should have been returning to its lair to rest during the heat of the day?

Oh well, Joel could look after himself. He didn't need her to tell him to be careful. If anyone needed looking after it had to be she, for she had never had to look after herself in the bush. There

had always been someone there: her father, her
mother or an African servant who had instructed
her how to recognise the spoor of the different
animals, none of which she could now remember.

She heard a rumble of thunder in the distance
and made a face at the still sulking fire. If they
were going to have anything hot for breakfast, she
would have to cheer it up somehow. At least
there was no trouble in making up her mind what
to cook. Joel had bought some hens' eggs from
the Turkana, eggs so small that they looked more
like pigeons' eggs to her. There was no bacon, but
there was a small tin of ham. She would scramble
the eggs, she decided, and shred the ham into
them. There were a few pieces of flat bread left,
hard and stale, but better than nothing, and a few
fruits, some mangoes from the coast that were
scarcely ripe enough yet to eat, and a pawpaw
that was more than ready. Pippa sliced it into two,
scraping out the multitude of black seeds from the
centre of the delicious orange fruit.

Joel appeared just as she was breaking the eggs
into the pan. She eyed him nervously and looked
away again.

"Where've you been?" she demanded. "Did
you know there was a leopard up that tree over
there? You might have got yourself killed!"

"Would you have cared?" he asked, lifting an
eyebrow.

Pippa wrestled with the problem of keeping the
pan over the flame and the smoke out of her eyes
at the same time.

"Of course I'd have cared! I don't even know
where we are! How d'you suppose I'd have found

my way out of this wilderness by myself? You
brought me here; you can jolly well return me to
civilisation in one piece! How d'you like your
eggs? Well done, or very well done?"

He took the pan from her, kicking the fire
down below into a greater heat. "I can see I
needn't have worried about taking an unfair
advantage of you," he muttered.

"Oh, that! It happens from time to time when a
man and a woman find themselves alone together.
If you don't apologise, I won't either."

Joel regarded her through narrowed eyes. "Was
that all it was?" There was a touch of steel in his
voice that warned her to be careful how she
worded her reply.

She shrugged her shoulders. "I don't think
there's any point of making more of it than it was,
do you?"

Joel moved the eggs round the pan with an
efficient movement of his wrist. "You sound like
an experienced widow—sometimes." He flipped
the eggs round again. "Sometimes you give the
impression of having no experience in that line at
all. Which is it, Pippa?"

"You know which it is! I was married to Timothy for more than three years—"

"Ah yes, Timothy!" he said nastily. "I thought
we'd come back to him."

"He was quite a large part of my life until
recently," she reminded him.

"So you keep telling me," he mocked her.

Pippa glanced at him through her lashes. "I
don't know what you're getting at," she said at
last. "You know I was married to Timothy. You

knew it that day in Nairobi—not that it made any difference to you. It doesn't matter to you whether your women are married or not, does it?"

"It matters!" He turned the eggs out onto the two tin plates she had put out ready beside the fire. "You've never felt like a married woman to me. You looked at me as if you'd never been kissed properly before, let alone wedded and bedded by the man you love."

Pippa accepted her plate of eggs with a wan smile. "It was such a brief meeting," she taunted him. "How could you possibly tell all that about me? I must say you have a lively imagination and a lot of gall if you think I thought twice about you—"

"Pippa!"

She shrugged her shoulders. "It didn't mean a thing! Oh, I admit you're an attractive man, but I never thought of you as anything other than a friend of my father's—"

"No?"

She glared at him. "No!"

He laughed shortly. "That isn't what you said the other day. Run as hard as you like, Pippa darling, you'll still come back for more. You won't change things by denying your own nature. You don't need my ring on your finger to make you mine."

"I don't belong to anyone!" she began angrily.

Joel tackled his plateful of eggs with zest. "Okay, we'll leave it there for now. We'll get to the national park today; what are you going to do then?"

Her fingers felt stiff as she played with her own

eggs. "I ought to take the Landrover back to Nairobi. What are you doing?"

"I'll fly down to Tsavo. Come with me and you could visit your mother for a while."

Pippa was startled out of her miserable contemplation of her immediate future. "My mother won't want to see me. She didn't like Timothy. She never forgave me for marrying him. And after . . . after Timothy's book, she cut us right out of her life. She doesn't want to have anything to do with me."

"Does she know Timothy is dead?"

Pippa shrugged her shoulders. "I don't know. I didn't tell her."

"Then it's time you did. She's down at the coast, trying to get the authorities to agree to her excavating some of the lost Swahili-Arab cities—"

"You've seen her recently?" Pippa accused him.

"She's a friend of mine, as your father was. She's a nice person. Go and see her, Pippa. It was never you that she wanted nothing more to do with; it was the company you kept."

"Perhaps," Pippa acknowledged. "But I never did know her very well. She took me once to Gedi with her when I was a child. I remember her reciting yards of Swahili poetry and expecting me to get as excited as she was about it, only I couldn't understand a word of it. Gedi is a very strange place. It's the only silent spot I know in Africa. Not a bird sings—nothing! All there is is the ruins of the medieval city, and I wasn't much interested in ruins at that age."

"You spent more time with your father?"

"I spent most of my time at school. My parents were very much in love with each other, but their work was always taking them apart from each other. When I was home, I was almost always in the way." Her chin firmed and tilted upwards. "I swore it would be different when I got married! I wanted to be with my husband all the time!"

A muscle jerked in Joel's cheek. "Your mother misses your father badly. Go and see her, Pippa. You may find things are different now."

Pippa finished her eggs, swallowing down the last of them with difficulty. "I'll have to take the Landrover back first. I'm serious about doing a biography of my father, you know. I have one or two interviews lined up in the next few days—"

"Your mother knew him better than anyone else. You'll have to go and see her sometime."

"I'll write to her," Pippa compromised.

"When?"

"I don't know when! I've got my own memories of my father to get straight first."

"Okay, but don't put it off too long," he warned her. "It won't get any easier to admit she was right about your marriage."

"I don't admit she was right!" Pippa stormed back at him.

He sat back on his heels and grinned at her. "She'll know the minute she sees you. Of course, if I were there with you, she might be less inclined to say she told you so. Doesn't that tempt you to fly down with me?"

"No. I have my own work to do!"

He stood up slowly, still looking mightily pleased with himself. "I could change your mind for you, but I have my work to do too, unfortunately. The elephants will be on the move soon and we'll have to go with them. Which will you do, the washing-up or striking the tent?"

Pippa chose the washing-up as being the easier task. She had never mastered how to put a frame tent together and she didn't think taking it apart would be any less of a muddle of canvas and tubes of aluminium. Besides, she was able to watch Joel's every movement as she swilled their few plates and pieces of cutlery through what was left over of the hot water. She wiped each article with care and stowed them away in the bag that fitted into the Landrover beside the haversack that carried all the food.

She liked looking at Joel. He moved with such an economy of movement, managing to reduce the tent to a neat pile of canvas and another of angular bits of frame that went into a second bag in a matter of a few moments. It had been just the same when he had put it up, she remembered. The only thing she had helped with was the inner compartment that had to be hung from the frame before the canvas was pulled over the top.

Joel turned his head unexpectedly and caught her staring at him.

"Enjoying the view?" he taunted her.

"Why not?" she returned casually. "You're not above doing the same."

She walked haughtily away from him, swinging the two bags from her fingers as she made her way across to the Landrover. When she gained the vehicle, she found he was right behind her.

"What d'you want?" she asked him.

His expression was stern and his eyes were bright with a gleam in them she didn't quite like. It was a look that made her uncomfortable and set her heart thudding against her ribs. With an effort she forced herself to look cool and as if she hadn't a care in the world.

"You know what I want, Pippa. I want you to come to Tsavo with me. I can't let you go back to Nairobi until I know what it is that makes you hold back from me."

She turned her back to him. "Like you, I have work to do!"

His hands caught her by the shoulders, his fingers digging into her flesh with a bruising force.

"I want you." The harshness of his voice made her shudder inwardly, though with what emotion she couldn't make up her mind. "And what's more, you want me too. As a widow, even Timothy's widow, it shouldn't be too difficult for you to see the advantage of us spending some more time together. You'd be all right with me."

She shut her eyes, concentrating all her efforts on standing up straight and not leaning back against his strength and letting it all happen to her.

"I think I'm better off as I am," she said at last. "Being widowed doesn't change the habits of a lifetime. Besides, what would my mother think if I arrived on her doorstep with a lover in tow? She'd show me the door even faster than she did before!"

"I wonder." Joel sounded amused. "Your mother has always seemed to me to be a most understanding woman—"

"You're not her daughter!" Pippa remembered the look in her mother's eyes when she had first introduced her to Timothy and had told her that this was the man she wanted to marry. She swung round to face Joel. "You think you can twist any woman round your little finger, don't you? I shouldn't advise you to try it with the Walker women, however. We have minds of our own!"

"Is that so?" he drawled. "Then why care if your mother knows we are lovers?"

"We're not lovers!"

"Not yet."

"We're not likely to be!" She raised her chin and glared at him in unconscious provocation. "If you'd been going to seduce me, you would have done it by now. The only reason you haven't is because you know we'd both live to regret it! We haven't got a thing in common—"

"Liar!"

"It's no more than the truth!" she declared indignantly.

He threw back his head and laughed, but there was no amusement in his laughter. "The only reason I haven't made love to you yet is because I can't get it out of my head you don't know what you're doing. Do you, Pippa?"

She gulped. "Of course I do!"

"Then there's nothing to stop us making the most of tonight, is there? Tomorrow, I'll go on to Tsavo and you can carry on to Nairobi. All right?"

"I don't know!" she said in a voice of desperation.

His hands pushed her T-shirt up her back,

stroking the smooth, silky skin of her back with gentle fingers.

"You've got all day to make up your mind. You can give me your answer tonight. One quick kiss, my love, and then we'd better get after those elephants."

Pippa looked vaguely about her and saw the elephants had indeed moved away from the water-hole, the Empress well out in front as she marshalled her followers for the day's march.

"Joel, there's something I ought to tell you—"

"Not now. You can tell me tonight, in my bed, when I've got you safely in my arms and there won't be any goats, or anything else, to disturb us."

She wished she could make a joke of it as he did, but memories of other nights got in her way. Timothy had called her frigid. Perhaps she would be with Joel, too. She had no way of knowing.

"It'll be too late tonight," she said sadly.

He wasn't listening, however. She could see her own image in the black centres of his eyes, but there was no clue there as to what he really thought of her.

"We'd better go," she said with a sigh.

"In a moment." His hands tightened on her back, pushing her so hard against him her breasts were crushed against the hard wall of his chest. "My, Pippa, you don't know what you do to me!"

His lips played with hers, brushing them apart. For a short while, it was enough for her to move her mouth against his at the same leisurely pace, but then a wave of desire hit her in the solar-plexus with an urgency that made her tighten her grasp on his neck and shoulders, her whole being centred on the relief she sought from his body against hers.

He was as shaken as she when he took a reluctant step away from her. She watched, fascinated, as he bent his back and picked up the two Hessian bags that held the tent and threw them into the Landrover, brushing his hands together to keep them from trembling as hers were. Memories played in her mind like old films, none of them seeming quite real to her. Joel wasn't Timothy, as he had said. It wasn't disappointment that had made him push her away and that brought a glow of triumph through her body. She made her way round the Landrover and climbed into the passenger seat, pulling her T-shirt demurely down and tucking it into the top of her jeans.

"Come on, Joel," she called out to him. "The Empress is getting impatient."

He got in beside her, slanting a smile in her direction. "So am I," he advised her dryly. "I'll fall apart if you don't say yes tonight, or something very like it, d'you know that?"

She chewed thoughtfully on her lower lip, wishing the hours away. He let in the clutch and the Landrover jerked forward over the rough ground. She didn't think it now, but she knew she was in love with Joel Buchanan, and whatever happened that night there would be no going back on that.

Chapter Six

It was late in the afternoon when they finally arrived at the national park. Pippa waited in the Landrover as Joel signed them in, exchanging a stream of banter with the smart *askari* on the gate.

"He says I'll be in trouble for losing that aeroplane," he said as he got back into the Landrover. "It's the second write-off this week. The Minister for Wild Life will be going spare. Very funny, he thought it, to get one's machine stamped on by an angry elephant. What was I doing? Arguing with you, I said. Aha, another example of the way females stick together! He seems to think you and the Empress were in cahoots to get me into hot water. How d'you like that?"

Pippa laughed. "I hope you didn't tell him I

didn't even know the Empress was a cow. I
thought her the biggest, angriest bull I'd ever
seen. I was scared stiff!"

"Wise girl! I've known the Empress for a good
many years now, but I wouldn't have taken any
liberties with her in that mood. She's still a wild
animal."

Pippa remembered how he had stood between
her and the angry elephant and had talked to the
enormous animal, calming her down. She had
accepted it then, unsurprised by anything that
Joel might do, but now she realised that they both
could easily have been killed.

She leaned back lazily, turning her face towards
him. "I didn't thank you for turning away her
wrath, did I?"

"I didn't want your thanks. There's always
been only one thing I want from you—and you
know it!"

She had no answer to that. Instead, she
changed the subject, looking about her with interest.

"I haven't been to one of the national parks
since I was a small child," she told him. "It
doesn't look any different from the surrounding
countryside, does it?"

"Wait until you see the Lodge. It isn't like the
old days when one could camp out in one of the
compounds put aside for the purpose. Now it's all
first-class hotels and luxury living."

Pippa smiled at the disapproval in his voice.
She remembered her own sense of disappointment when her father had taken her for the day to
the great Amboseli Reserve and they had spent

most of their time eating an enormous lunch in a
building that wouldn't have looked out of place in
Nairobi. There had been a gorgeous view from
the windows, stretching right over the water-hole
and salt-lick that had been devised to attract the
animals. But it hadn't seemed anything like the
stories her father had told her of his boyhood,
when it had been common to sleep out under
canvas and be awoken in the night by a rhinoceros
scratching itself on a post and bringing the whole
tent down around its occupant's ears.

"I'll settle for a bath," she said aloud.

"And an early night?"

She blushed. She was trying not to think as far
as that. Every time she made up her mind that
one night with Joel was worth the misery of
parting from him the morning after, she would
remember Timothy's contempt for her and decide
that she simply didn't have the courage to go
through with it.

"Maybe," she said.

"It isn't too late to come to Tsavo with me."

She bit her lip, not looking at him. "I have to
do the biography of my father first."

"He never blamed you for anything. Why
blame yourself?"

"I thought Timothy had integrity and deserved
my loyalty—"

Joel hit the palm of his hand against the driving-
wheel. "If you ask me, you were afraid of him,"
he interrupted her.

"I've never been afraid of anyone!"

"Maybe not," he grunted. "One of these days
you'll have to tell me about your marriage to Mr.

Gregson. You'll feel a lot better when you've got it all off your chest.''

"Says who?" she jeered.

"If you don't want to tell me, tell your mother!"

She froze at the thought. "It's water under the bridge. Timothy's dead, so what good would it do?"

"Ah, so there is something that's still bugging you about him! I thought so!"

"Not about him," she denied. "About myself, maybe."

He frowned, glancing sideways at her. "Maybe it's as well he's dead," he said grimly. "I was tempted to wring his neck for him in Nairobi. I wouldn't be able to keep my hands off him now. You were always too good for him!"

"He didn't think so!" The words were out before she could stop them and were regretted as quickly. "It could be you're prejudiced," she added, to cover up her mistake.

"It could be, but I don't think so. I mean to find out tonight."

"Don't count your chickens before they're hatched," she warned him.

"I won't," he promised, but she knew he thought that she was as eager as he to give him this one night in her life. He didn't seem to care that they might never see each other again.

The Lodge came into view quite suddenly. Joel pointed it out to her, or Pippa wouldn't have seen it even then, for the round rondavels that were the guest rooms merged into the dry, yellow-grey landscape as if they had always been there. It was only when they came closer and she was able to pick out the sturdier wooden frame of the public rooms that she was convinced they really had arrived.

The Lodge had been built on the edge of a cliff, with the water-hole and salt-lick placed down below and lit by some huge spot-lights she would have thought guaranteed to keep all but the bravest of the animals away.

"Do they really turn those on at night?" she enquired.

"Only after most of the animals have gone. The honey-badgers don't seem to mind them, and they only come out late at night."

"Are they badgers?" Pippa asked him.

"Nothing like them, except for a few stripes round their heads. These are truly vicious animals. Their real name is ratel."

Pippa wasn't much wiser. She had lived in Kenya all her life, yet she didn't feel that she knew all that much about it. The school's syllabus had come straight from England and, in theory, she knew much more about that country than she did her own. Perhaps her mother had had a point, after all, when she had wanted her to appreciate some of the great Swahili poetry from the coastal region.

There was a moment when the Lodge looked more like a prison than a tourist attraction, for here, in the national parks, it was the animals who walked free, while the humans were kept safely behind barriers. There were notices by the entrance, warning visitors not to stray outside the Lodge limits and one or two graphic photographs of what had happened to one or two fools who had tried it. Of course, Pippa knew herself to be in less danger than was somebody who was there on holiday only. After a few years, a white man, as easily as a black one, can acquire the local smell that makes them less irritating to the predators that stalk over the plains, living the life they have always lived, with only man as a danger to their continued existence.

Joel dropped Pippa off at the reception desk, carrying her few belongings into the darkened, glass-enclosed area.

"Mind if I go on borrowing your Landrover for a while? I have to report to the warden and make sure the elephants are settling in. I'll have someone check it over and return it to the hirers in Nairobi for you—"

"I may drive it down tomorrow," Pippa interrupted him.

"Not on your own, you don't! If you insist on going, there's bound to be a plane going sometime."

Pippa clenched her teeth. "I prefer to make my own arrangements!"

He cupped her chin in the palm of his hand. "That doesn't stop me worrying about you, my love. It's a small favour to ask of you, surely, that you should fly down to Nairobi and not have that gruelling journey on your own?" He bent his head and brushed his lips softly over hers. "I'll be back as soon as I can. You won't be lonely, will you?"

Pippa gulped. "No." She felt quite faint just thinking about it. "But, Joel, I'm not—"

"Tell me later, love!"

Pippa's hand was still shaking when she signed the register and was allotted a room for the night. She didn't think she'd have the courage to go through with it, but how could she not? Perhaps they could talk over dinner? But, no, there was bound to be somebody that one of them knew in the dining-room. She would make time afterwards, when they were drinking their coffee and watching the antics of the honey-badgers, or she'd put it off until later still. . . .

"Mrs. Gregson?"

Pippa brought her mind back to the present with difficulty. "I'm sorry, what did you say?"

"I see you have some of Mr. Buchanan's things with yours. Shall I have them put in his room?"

"It doesn't matter. Does he have a room already?"

The black face broke into a wide smile. "He always has the same room when he's here. It's the next one along from yours. They have the best view of the water-hole in the whole Lodge!"

Pippa hoped she looked considerably cooler and more sophisticated than she felt at that moment. She cleared her throat and murmured a polite thank you, but the receptionist wasn't finished with her yet.

"Shall I reserve a table for you and Mr. Buchanan tonight? You don't want to have to share with another couple, do you?"

"I don't care either way," Pippa assured him.

She thought the man looked disappointed.

"What does Mr. Buchanan generally do?" she asked him.

The smile was back on his face. "Don't worry, *memsahib*, it'll be the best table we have!"

Pippa looked at him helplessly. "Thank you," she said.

Alone in her room, she looked about her expectantly, though what she was looking for she couldn't have told. She busied herself with her unpacking, wondering what to wear for dinner that evening, though she kept telling herself that it didn't matter, Joel wouldn't notice what she wore. In the end she decided on a silky-looking dress in a paisley design that she seldom wore and didn't much care for herself in. She put it on and took it off again, wishing she had her entire wardrobe with her. There was nothing else suitable that she had with her. There was a soft cream dress that had a tie at the throat and waist, but the dust had got into her case and it looked a mess. With a sigh, she put the despised paisley dress on again and began to think it wasn't so bad after all.

When she had finished doing her hair and making up her face, she went out before she could change her mind again, locking the door behind her. If she hurried, she thought, she'd be in time to order some tea. She could sit comfortably by the window overlooking the water-hole and pretend to read some of the tourist magazines that had been left on one of the tables.

She was still sipping her first cup when Joel came to join her. Some instinct warned her of his presence and she looked up just in time to see him striding over to where she was sitting.

"That looks like a good idea," he said easily. "Mind if I send for another cup?"

"Of course not."

He looked her up and down, a slight smile in his eyes. "You look good enough to eat!" he told her.

The colour rushed up into her face. "In this? I'm not very fond—I mean, it doesn't really suit me—"

"What makes you think that?"

She lifted her shoulders, chewing her lower lip. "Nobody's ever liked it," she told him.

"You must have when you bought it." He sat down beside her, stretching his long legs out in front of him.

"That was a long time ago," she murmured. She studied him over the rim of her cup for a bit and then went on in a rush, "It hasn't very happy associations for me."

"Tell me about it," he invited her.

"I wanted to look older—more sophisticated— when I bought it. Timothy said I looked ridiculous in it."

Some of the pain she had felt then lingered in her voice despite her efforts to keep her tone light and uncaring. It had been her "going-away dress," and she had worn it proudly, excited by her new status as a married woman. It had been the first of the many rejections she had suffered that day, and perhaps that was why she remembered it with such bitterness.

"If I told you how I think you look we'd have to adjourn either to your bedroom or mine." The glint in his eyes made her sit up with a jerk. She held her breath, a small pulse beating frenetically at the base of her neck. "That might be a good idea anyway," he added quietly. "If we don't do anything else, we could talk."

She replaced her cup in its saucer with immense dignity. "I don't want to talk!" she said abruptly. "I'm quite happy where I am."

His expression softened, but the glint was still there, a very male glint that made her tingle from head to foot.

"Okay, I can wait, my Pippa. I hear you've ordered a secluded table for us tonight. What are your plans after that?"

"I—you—I haven't got any."

His gaze swept over her, settling on the curve of her breasts and then on her hastily licked lips. "You can't go on running away for ever, my love. There'll still be time for you to change your mind and come with me to Tsavo tomorrow."

Fortunately, a wave of anger came to Pippa's rescue. "I've told you I'm not going with you. I have my own work to do, work that's important to me! How would you feel if I asked you to give Tsavo a miss and come to Nairobi with me?"

"I'd take it as a compliment. Are you asking me to go with you?"

Pippa got to her feet, getting a twenty-shilling note out of her purse to pay for the tea. "No, of course not!" she declared violently. She walked slowly out of the room without a single backward glance.

Dinner passed in a dream. Pippa had no idea what she ate, conscious only of the man seated opposite her and how well he looked in a formal cream suit, his shirt freshly ironed and his tie tied to perfection. She had some idea that the food was worthy of any good city restaurant and wondered how they achieved such style miles from anywhere, when most of the ingredients probably had to be flown up from Nairobi.

When the waiter brought their coffee, grinning all over his face at the sight of Mr. Buchanan exchanging small talk with this strange woman, she knew the moment of truth had come.

Joel cocked an eyebrow at her. "Well, what is it to be?"

She almost choked over the last of her coffee. "Give me half an hour," she whispered. "I'll come to your room."

She didn't know what she had expected from him, but it was something more than an impassive nod of his head, which was all she got. She surveyed him with increasing irritation and then turned her attention to the darkness outside, the sounds of the African night, half hoping to catch a glimpse of the promised honey-badgers.

Even as she was looking, the lights came on outside and an African ran out, laying a trail of meat to bring the ratels closer to the waiting guests. He ran back inside faster still, stressing how dangerous these animals could be. They had claws like razors and teeth to match, tearing their victim to shreds in a few moments.

Viewed through a toughened pane of glass, however, they seemed cuddly and rather sweet as they waddled about, wolfing down the meat and looking for more. They did look rather like badgers, Pippa thought, though bigger. They were rather beautiful, with their distinctive stripes and black-and-white faces.

"Your half an hour is slipping away," Joel warned her after a few moments.

Pippa sent him a look of unconscious appeal but, apart from a slight tightening of his mouth, he seemed not to notice. For a ghastly instant of time, she thought she was going to faint and almost welcomed the idea. She wasn't going to be able to see this through. She was frightened, scared of Joel and even more scared of herself.

"I'm going," she muttered.

Her night-clothes had been bought for the single life. She tossed them over the bed, not really seeing them at all. What did it matter what she wore? She chose a cotton nighty, smocked by herself, which at least had some kind of style, and pulled it over her head, viewing herself in the glass as she did so. She looked more like a young innocent than ever! Oh well, her dressing-gown would change that, she hoped. Made from terry-towelling, it was unisex in design and could easily have belonged to Timothy at one time.

It was the hardest thing she had ever done in her life to shut and lock her own door and walk along the corridor to Joel's. She raised her hand to announce her arrival with a knock, when it was snatched open and Joel pulled her inside at a speed that rendered her breathless.

"Now you're here, I don't want you changing your mind again," he said grimly. "You're here to stay!"

Pippa said nothing at all. When he lifted her off her feet and sat her down on the edge of his bed, she went on sitting there, unable to move a muscle. Joel stood beside her, his legs touching hers, his hands on his hips as he looked at her.

"Is this how you made love to Timothy?"

Pippa's lips trembled and then she burst into tears, hiding her face behind her hands as she struggled to find the words to explain herself to Joel.

"I don't know how!" she burst out in the end.

It was like being in a slow-motion film. The pressure of his legs against hers increased as he bent over her, his hands grasping her shoulders in a painful grip.

"You are Timothy's widow, Mrs. Gregson, aren't you?"

There was a roaring in her ears brought on by sheer fright, but there was something else too: a bubble of excitement in her middle that was growing by the minute, building up to a shattering climax of need she had never experienced before. She flung her arms up round his neck and arched against him, longing for his kiss.

"You know I am," she said.

"I'm beginning to wonder, sweetheart. I can almost feel sorry for the fellow, whereas I only hated him before."

She clung to him harder than ever. "Why should you feel sorry for him?" she cried out. "Why don't you go on hating him?"

His mouth took hers in a punishing kiss that didn't begin to satisfy her. "I hated him because he had what I wanted, but he didn't have you, did he?"

Pippa stood in front of him, shaking. Was it

going to happen all over again? She wrenched
herself free from Joel's slackened embrace and
whirled over to the other side of the bed, safely
out of his reach.

"I don't know what you're talking about!" she
muttered angrily.

Joel followed her more slowly, cutting off her
retreat by catching her by the arm and flinging her
across the bed. He dived after her, the weight of
his body holding her quiescent beneath him.
More gently, he undid the cord of her gown,
pushing the garment out of his way.

"No? What happened between you and Timothy?"

"Nothing happened!" she said in despair.

He dropped a shower of kisses on her cheeks,
her nose and finally her lips. "Whose idea was
that?" he growled in his throat.

She put both hands against his chest, flexing her
muscles to push him away. "It wasn't mine!"

He allowed her to sit up, but his legs still held
her down onto the bed. She wriggled against him,
making no impression at all.

"Let me up," she demanded. "Just because
you're bigger than I am, don't think—"

"I don't!" His lips twitched. "Some widow-
woman you turned out to be! That poor guy—"

"I don't see why you have to feel so sorry for
him! What about me? It was me he turned out of
his bed, telling me I was frigid and unloving."

Joel's lips twitched again. "And you believed
him?"

"Yes, I did!" Her indignation mounted as she
began to wonder if she hadn't been a fool all

along. "I *was* cold and unloving! It got so I couldn't bear him to touch me!"

Joel's delighted laughter caught her mid-ribs. She stared at him as if she'd never seen him before. Her whole world changed perspective, and she could feel herself blushing from head to foot.

"It wasn't all his fault," she said. "I knew when he didn't like the dress that I'd made a mistake. I wasn't in love with him at all. He was there and I was lonely. I was always being sent somewhere out of the way, and I knew he wouldn't do that to me. He seemed so kind and gentle—"

Joel's fingers brushed her ear, tangling themselves in her hair. "Okay, sweetheart, you don't have to tell me any more. The problem is what are we going to do now?"

It didn't seem a problem at all to Pippa. She rubbed her fingers along his chin, noting with pleasure that he had taken the time to shave while he'd been waiting for her to come to him. She liked the feel of his rough skin and she began to explore further, a little bemused by her own daring.

"Make love to me," she invited him.

"That's the problem, sweetheart—"

"You don't want me!"

The tears stung at the back of her eyes and she was very much afraid that she was going to start crying again. It was too bad when she wanted him to think her an eager, responsive woman, the kind of woman he would want to make love to, even if he never saw her again.

"Of course I want you, you silly goose! Only

you're not the widow you claim to be." His mouth twisted into a wry smile. "I don't seduce innocent young women, no matter how desirable they may be—"

"Why not?"

"Because you might regret it afterwards and I couldn't bear that."

"Don't you mean you'd regret it? You think I may blackmail you into a relationship you don't want, but I won't! I—I just want you now, not for ever!"

He placed his hand over her heart and she thought she had won, but a moment later he had left her and was staring into the darkness out of the window.

"You don't know what you want, Pippa. It'll be different when you do. Go to Nairobi, do whatever you want, but promise me one thing. When you do know what you want, come and tell me what it is, will you?"

"I want you," she said simply, but she could tell he didn't believe her. Somehow, though, his rejection of her didn't hurt as much as she had thought it would. Someday, she'd make him love her, she promised herself, and she crossed her fingers for good luck. Third time lucky? She certainly hoped so. Joel was the most important thing in her life and there had to be some way of persuading him that she'd never amount to much without him.

"I'll go back to my own room," she said aloud. "Good night, Joel."

He didn't answer.

Chapter Seven

Pippa was cheerful the whole way to Nairobi. She hadn't seen Joel that morning, but her confidence in herself was unabated when she stepped into the tiny aeroplane that was to take her south. Sooner or later, she was sure that Joel would come looking for her again. All she had to do was get on with her biography of her father and wait.

She was a little less sure of ultimate success as she drove the short distance from the airport into the centre of the city. It may have been that she knew the taxi-driver was overcharging her, or it may have been the sudden sense of loneliness she felt as she approached the one place in the world she had always looked on as home, but where now she had no home of her own because it hadn't seemed worthwhile to keep on her apartment while she had been studying in London.

However it was, she was quite suddenly lonelier than she had ever been in her whole life.

The beauty of the city made little impression on her. She hardly noticed the mauve clouds of flowers of the jacaranda trees, or the brilliant shades of the bougainvillea bushes that lined the whole length of Kenyatta Avenue. In London, she had frequently boasted that all her friends who despised the monstrosities that were ruining the Western world in the name of modern architecture should all travel to Nairobi and see what could be done. Nairobi, in her opinion, was the most beautiful city in the world. Others had told her that Mexico City was better still, but she had never been there, and so she went right on thinking that Nairobi was the king-pin of them all. After all, there was no other capital city that had a national park in the suburbs, full of the animals for which East Africa was famous, or a museum that housed the remains of the very beginnings of mankind, made possible by people like the Leakeys and her father.

The taxi drew up outside the Pan-Afric Hotel and she roused herself to get out and go inside to book a room for the night. Her mood wasn't improved by the driver having no change and no inclination, either, to get any from the hotel.

"Wait there!" she ordered him, meaning to get some herself, but the man refused, not trusting her out of his sight.

"Okay, you tell me what we're going to do," she said crossly. "I'm not giving you all that for such a short ride."

By way of answer, he snatched the highest note

she had out of her hand and got back into the cab, slamming the door shut after him. Pippa was too furious to think of taking his number until it was too late and, by that time, there was nothing to be done but to go into the hotel.

The pretty receptionist was sympathetic but held out no hope of Pippa ever getting her money back. "You have to be careful in Nairobi these days," she warned. "They're calling us the Chicago of Africa and I don't think they mean it as a compliment."

Pippa was sure they didn't. She took the lift up to her room, the key with an animal carving attached to it dangling from one hand and her suitcase in the other. She felt quite exhausted by the journey and disoriented by the sudden change of scene. It was quite an effort to settle herself into her room and make the telephone calls for the appointments she needed to get information for her book.

Ten minutes after she had replaced the receiver after the last call, she had made up her mind she was in the wrong place at the wrong time and went through the whole list, cancelling all the arrangements she had just finished making.

Downstairs again, she enquired into flights down to the coast and was told there would be no difficulty in getting to Malindi that evening. The receptionist was as nice as ever.

"Why don't you have some lunch, Mrs. Gregson, while I book your ticket for you. It's no trouble. Your mother will be pleased to see you, I'm sure."

"How did you know I was going to visit her?" she enquired.

"She rang up earlier asking if you'd arrived safely."

"My mother did?"

"Why, yes, Mrs. Gregson. You were making a telephone call out of the hotel at that moment and she said it didn't matter not speaking to you personally, but to jog your mind that she was still in the land of the living. She sounded nice."

"She is," Pippa agreed, "but busy."

"You seem pretty busy yourself," the receptionist answered with a smile. "I'll let you know what time your flight leaves, shall I? I expect it'll be at about tea-time, so you've plenty of time to have lunch and a short nap afterwards."

Pippa did as the girl suggested, managing to fall asleep for an hour or two, which made her feel worse than ever, because she wasn't accustomed to sleeping in the daytime. A short time later she was on her way back to the airport, and she took her place on the scheduled flight to Mombasa and Malindi.

It was interesting coming down at Mombasa. Mombasa Island, joined to the mainland by a bridge and a causeway, was clearly visible, looking green and lush. There was a story that the island was a part of a fallen star, which she had always believed as a child. Mombasa had always seemed like a steamy, romantic paradise to her.

Shortly afterwards they took off again for the short hop to Malindi, some forty miles up the coast. It was almost dark when Pippa went through the formalities required to hire a Mini-Moke to drive herself round the small resort and set off through the Old Town, down Harambee Road, the unassuming main street, looking for the house where she had been told her mother was staying.

The familiar sights of the mango packers and the plain Borora Mosque told her she was on the right road. She hurried on before it got really dark and before she began to wish she had hired an enclosed vehicle for her visit. The Vasco da Gama Monument came up on her left, followed by the typically British Colonial architecture of the Council Offices, complete with a flame-tree on the grounds.

As she slowed the car, she caught sight of the only house around, set well back from the road, and turned the Moke into the drive, parking it neatly under the trees not far from the front door. An African servant came to the door in answer to her knock, a white Muslim cap perched on the back of his head. Although Pippa asked for her mother in Swahili, he was proud of his English and preferred to ask her to come inside in that language.

"Mrs. Walker has just come in. May I see if she is receiving anyone before she has her bath? Whom shall I say has called?"

"I'm Pippa Gregson, Mrs. Walker's daughter."

His jaw sagged. "From Nairobi? Are you staying the night, *memsahib?*"

"I hope so," Pippa said. She felt clammy from head to foot, which may have been due to the sudden change from the considerable height of

Nairobi to the humid heat of sea level. It was always a dry heat up country, giving a large part of Kenya one of the best climates in the world.

The African disappeared and Pippa heard her mother's excited exclamation, followed by the sound of her running feet as she came into the hall to greet her.

"My darling girl, come in and let me have a good look at you! I'm so happy you're here! I thought you had business in Nairobi—"

"I had, but it didn't seem so terribly important any longer. I wanted to see you. Do you mind?"

"Mind? Pippa, you always did get the most extraordinary ideas into your head for no reason at all. Why should I mind anything so delightful?"

Pippa released herself from her mother's awkward embrace, smiling to herself. "You could hardly bring yourself to say anything to me the last time I saw you," she reminded her.

"Not you, dear. Timothy. But that's all over, I gather?"

"Yes. I thought you knew? Kenya's a small place when it comes to gossip, and there was quite a lot when he went rushing off to South Africa."

"I never listen to gossip," her mother declared virtuously. And it was true, she never had. In Pippa's experience, she had never listened at all, having far too many other things on her mind.

"Timothy was killed."

"Well, one shouldn't wish him dead of course, but it does solve most of your problems, doesn't it? You can tell me all about it over a drink. You're staying to dinner, I hope?"

"I planned to stay a few nights as well if that's all right?" her daughter returned.

"Tonight is quite all right, my dear, but I'm off to Lamu tomorrow. You can come with me if you like, but I can't guarantee to give you my full attention while we're there. You know how it is."

Pippa knew exactly. A year ago, she would have been devastated by her mother's indifferent invitation, quite sure that she was trying to get her out of the way for some reason of her own. Now, she had grown up enough to catch the concern that lay beneath her mother's words and to know her welcome was a real one, although it would probably never be put into words.

"I'd like that." She hesitated. "Mother, I'm sorry Timothy—" She swallowed. "I'm writing a biography of Daddy, hoping to put things right. I have a publisher in London—"

"I'll be interested to read it," her mother cut her off. "Do I gather your obsessive loyalty to that disagreeable husband of yours died when he did?"

"Shortly afterwards," Pippa admitted.

"Then we can be friends again. I've been told you went through a bad time with that terrible man. I wish you'd told me and we might have been rid of him sooner. Were you dreadfully unhappy?"

"Yes, I was."

"But it's all right now?"

Pippa nodded. "I went to London for a while. I haven't been back in Kenya long. I went up to the Northern Territory to see the place where Daddy found the skull."

"So I heard."

"You did? I thought you never listened to gossip?"

Her mother smiled. "You're looking tired, darling. An early night for both of us, I think?"

Pippa knew her mother would probably never mention Timothy to her again, and she felt a vast relief that it was all over at last and they were friends again.

"It'll be fun going to Lamu with you," she said aloud.

Her mother put her head on one side, her eyes twinkling. "Have you ever been there before? I can't remember. A friend has lent me his house, so we won't have to go back and forth, at least. It's a long, long time since we visited Gedi together, isn't it? Lamu is far more interesting, of course, because it's alive and Gedi is dead. The people fascinate me."

"I thought you preferred dead places!" Pippa exclaimed.

"Certainly not!" her mother denied. "They're only fun if you have the imagination—and the knowledge—to people them properly. I have both. As a child you had neither, but I'm hoping for better things from you now that you seem to have finally turned into an adult human-being. I've never known what to say to children of the species."

"And you didn't like Timothy?"

A muscle jerked in the older woman's face. "There's a very interesting saying in the Bible, my dear, that advises one to let the dead bury the dead. If I were you, I'd let Timothy rest in peace, and I'd get on with the exciting business of living. Our time in this world is terribly short and you've wasted enough of your life already on someone who was dead to the real business of living from the moment he was born. I just hope you'll do better next time. You can hardly do worse!"

Pippa managed a wry laugh. "I haven't got your powers of concentration, or your certainty that I've got my priorities right. You and Daddy always knew exactly what you wanted to do and how to go about it—"

Mrs. Walker shook her head. "Is that how we seemed to you? I remember it as one long compromise as we struggled to do all the things we both wanted to do. I hated not being with him all the time. He was the most exciting man I've ever known."

Joel was exciting too! Pippa fought down the tremor of anticipation that surfaced whenever Joel came to mind. It was as if he had tied invisible cords around her heart and gave them a jerk every now and again to remind her that he hadn't given up on her yet.

"You never thought of giving up your own career?" she asked.

"No, never!" her mother answered. "We both knew I'd be unbearable if I did. My work is as much a part of me as your father's was of him. You're lucky, if you're going to take up writing biographies. You can do that anywhere!"

Anywhere? Pippa wondered if her mother had any idea of what was involved in interviewing people and visiting relevant places, all of which was necessary to laying the foundations for a sound life of someone.

"One biography will be enough for me," she said dryly. "I'll try my hand at fiction after that."

"Good idea!" said her mother.

It had always been the same when Mrs. Walker had set out anywhere: Either she took with her everything she owned, or she did what she called travelling light, which meant she took nothing at all, not even the bare essentials. The only things she thought she'd need in Lamu were a notebook and a ball-point pen.

"The house where we're going has everything we could possibly need for such a short time. What have you got in that bag, Pippa?"

"*My* notebook," Pippa told her.

Her mother shrugged. "I should have thought you could have carried most of it in your head. And what's that?"

"A cassette recorder."

"Well, you won't need that!"

"I still have to talk to you about Daddy," Pippa reminded her. "Who knew him better than you did?"

"I won't say a word if you're going to take it all down on that," her mother said firmly. "It would be like talking to one of those gadgets that answer the phone for you."

"No, it won't. It'll be like talking to me. Honestly, Mother, I'm not going to leave anything behind, so let's go, shall we?"

Mrs. Walker maintained a haughty distance the

whole way up the coast. Only when they boarded the small native boat that was to take them across to the island did she lower her dignity sufficiently to say, "Now you'll regret all that luggage you've brought with you! I'm not going to carry any of it for you!"

"I expect I shall manage," she said.

"There are no cars on the island," her mother told her. "The streets are too narrow. We'll have to walk to the house—and everywhere else for that matter."

"Good," said Pippa. "I like walking."

Travelling to Lamu was like entering a time-machine and emerging some five centuries earlier. Nothing had changed since the days when the Portuguese Vasco da Gama had discovered the coast of East Africa for Europe five hundred years before. Not much had changed since even earlier times, when Marco Polo had started on his great journey to China and when the famous Chinese eunuch sea captains were already travelling vast distances in the interests of their country's trade.

The streets were narrow, but they led in and out of vast, open squares where most of the life of the island was lived. Pippa was inclined to linger. She enjoyed looking at the groups of men, who were dressed in long white robes and beautifully embroidered Muslim caps. She also speculated about the women, who were shrouded from head to foot in universal black, with only glimpses of their gold jewellery betraying the wealth of many of the local families.

"Hurry up, dear, do! I knew you'd find those bags too heavy!"

"Mother—"

Mrs. Walker summoned two small boys from across the road to take the bags from her daughter, pleased with herself for having been proved right in her own eyes, at least. Pippa sighed, relinquishing her burden with reluctance, because the cassette recorder was a good one and she didn't want to lose it. Judging by the set of her mother's back as she walked swiftly up the narrow, sandy lane, there was no point in arguing the matter further. Pippa scowled after her retreating figure.

At the end of the small street, her mother paused, looking back over her shoulder. "We're here!" she announced.

Pippa took her bags back from the boys, gesturing towards her mother when they looked expectantly at her for their tip. It wasn't often that she had ever got the better of her mother, and she could hardly refrain from laughing as her mother groped for the coppers and her key.

It grated in the lock and the door was opened to them. Inside it was dark and cool, and the two women stepped over the threshold with a slight shiver as they left the humid heat behind them outside.

"What a lovely house!" Pippa exclaimed.

"Isn't it? I believe it's one of the oldest on the island, though as they were all built in much the same way for hundreds of years, it's difficult to date it exactly."

This was her mother at her best, Pippa reflected, as the older woman pointed out the outer blocks of coral rag, and how the roof was supported on beams of hard wood brought over from the mainland.

"Very necessary, when you consider that the roof's made of sandstone and coral. Another consequence of having to keep up all that weight is that the rooms are long and narrow, though they've managed to make them look more spacious by the lavishness of the beautiful plaster work and the clever proportions. I never feel at all crowded when I'm here."

Pippa hoped she didn't. It was like living in a palace. She looked about her, admiring the intricacy of the plaster work, noting the strong Arab influence that not only made the rooms a pleasure to look at but also governed their original usage. The public rooms were for the men, whilst the women, the heart of every Moslem household, had been allocated the cooler and therefore more pleasant apartments upstairs where they could catch any breeze that was going.

"I thought you'd like it," her mother said, not without satisfaction.

"I do!"

"Enough to be curious about its owner?"

"I suppose so," Pippa admitted. The truth was that she hadn't given a thought as to whose house it was. Both her parents had always had a great number of influential friends of all kinds and, ever since she could remember, she had been writing to one or another of them at the strangest addresses, sometimes the highest and sometimes the lowest in the land.

"Well, I'm not going to tell you about him. You'll find out soon enough for yourself who he is." She glanced at her watch, her eyes flickering with irritation. "It's too late to do anything much today—thanks to your dawdling all the way here! They'll be serving a meal at any moment, and there's no point in absenting myself from that because everybody else on the island will be doing the same. Never mind, it'll give you time to tell me about your book. Shall we go into the sitting room, or would you rather go upstairs to one of the bedrooms?"

"Wherever you like," Pippa answered her.

Her mother sniffed the air expectantly. "Curry! Good. As I can't go out, I've decided I'm hungry. I hope they hurry up with it."

She led the way through a small reception room into the elaborate *salamlik,* furnished now with a desk, a couple of divans piled high with cushions and, as a concession to Western joints, a couple of spindly chairs forged out of some kind of metal and painted white.

Mrs. Walker sank down onto one of the divans, pulling the cushions into a comfortable nest all around her. She looked at her watch again.

"We've got a few minutes. What makes you think anyone will want to read about Joe's life?"

Pippa sat down also. "I wanted to put the record straight."

"Last time I saw you, you hadn't a doubt that Timothy was telling the truth. What changed your mind?"

"Last time you saw me I was married to Timothy. Nobody was on his side except me. You all disliked him so much that you never gave him a chance—"

"Didn't it ever occur to you that we had good reason to dislike him?"

"Perhaps. Not at first, but later on. I was still his wife, however."

"You were Joe's daughter too."

"I still am. Writing about him is the best I can do to put things right. Timothy's dead, so it can't hurt him now. While he was alive, I thought I owed it to him. I know you think I was wrong—"

"Of course you were wrong! There wasn't any question about it. I couldn't believe that you'd shilly-shally about with the truth like that! *My* daughter putting her sentimental feelings for that wretched little toad of a man before what you had to know to be the truth! I said to your father, if we'd taught you so little about facing facts with a modicum of objectivity, we had completely failed you as parents! He said he didn't think you had anything else to give Timothy. He was always more tolerant than I!"

"He was right," Pippa said sadly. "I had nothing Timothy wanted, nothing at all."

"You're a fool!" her mother told her. "I can't think what you ever saw in him."

"I was lonely."

"Lonely?" Her mother sat bolt upright. "How could you have been lonely? I'm sure I was always pointing out to you what marvellous things you could do with your time if you'd only brought yourself to concentrate on something that interested you. Heaven knows, Joe and I gave you a very good example in that respect—"

"I wanted people! Or rather just one person who had time to talk and who wanted me with him."

Her mother's eyes rounded with astonishment. "We were always there, dear. Why didn't you say something?"

"It wasn't important compared to what you and Daddy were doing. But this book is important to me and I'm going to make a good job of it."

"D'you know what you're doing?" her mother asked doubtfully.

Pippa nodded and her quiet certainty got through to her mother, who shook her head at her and laughed suddenly. "I believe you do! I'll help all I can, darling, but it's no good expecting me to gloss over what Timothy did to Joe. I feel murderous whenever I think about it!"

"It'll be the truth, I promise you that, or as near to the truth as I can make it. It may not be exactly as you'd like it to be, either, but it certainly won't whitewash Timothy or anyone else."

Her mother smiled a wry little smile. "All right, darling, I'll settle for that. I can see that you're all grown up and that you're going to do it your way. I'll help all I can and I won't interfere if I can possibly help it. Where are you going to start?"

Pippa began to tell her the general plan of the book she had in her mind, elaborating on the years that her mother could most help her with. She felt at a disadvantage at first, expecting to be interrupted, put right and even laughed at for some of her ideas, and it was only slowly that she realised that her mother was really listening to her with the same respect that Pippa had seen her pay to other professionals in her own field and outside it.

"I'll need photographs—"

The rasping sound of the front-door being unlocked cut her off midstream. The two women looked round, waiting for the arrival of their host. Pippa heard a deep male laugh. There was only one man who sounded quite like that. It was Joel Buchanan.

Chapter Eight

One heart-stopping moment lengthened into another and still Pippa could do nothing but stare at Joel, unable to believe he was really there.

"I'm glad you came," he said at last.

The room swam before her eyes and slowly righted itself again.

"I didn't know this was your house," she breathed.

"I imagine not." He looked amused, as he so often was where she was concerned. "Your mother knew, however."

It would be some time before Pippa would forgive her for not sharing that bit of knowledge. She felt tricked.

"There wasn't much doing in Nairobi," she began to explain. "I flew down to the coast to see my mother. I didn't know you would be here."

"What was wrong with Nairobi?"

She thought of the appointments she had made and then cancelled and berated herself for her lack of discipline.

"I came to the conclusion that it was better to get the background information from my mother first." Her eyelids fluttered and she didn't dare look directly at him. "She knew my father better than anyone, after all."

Joel flung himself down on the divan beside her, possessing himself of her hand with an unselfconsciousness she wished she could emulate. She could think of nothing else but the interested look her mother gave them both, but when she tried to pull her hand away, his fingers fastened on hers all the more firmly, a slight smile turning up the corners of his mouth.

"You look well, Mrs. Walker," he addressed her mother. "What d'you think of Pippa's plan to write Joe's biography?"

"She ought to make a good job of it, though I doubt she'll make much money out of it. What are you living on, by the way, Pippa?"

"I have enough to get by for the moment. Later on I'll get a proper job and support myself. I don't want to be Timothy's widow for ever!"

Joel made a caustic noise at the back of his throat and exchanged glances with Mrs. Walker.

"Why don't you say it?" Pippa sighed.

"Oh, I think we all know the score," he answered her. "Or haven't you told your mother?"

"Told me what?" Mrs. Walker demanded.

Pippa favoured Joel with a furious look, snatch-

ing her hand out of his with a violence that told
volumes about her displeasure.

"That's my business!" she snapped.

Her mother looked vaguely into the middle
distance. "If it's about that impossible husband of
yours, I don't want to hear it. Joel, are we going
to eat soon? I'm absolutely famished. Never
travel anywhere with Pippa if you're in a hurry!
We only just got here ourselves, would you
believe that?"

"I don't see how we could have got here any
faster!" Pippa retorted.

"I'm surprised you ever get anywhere," Mrs.
Walker insisted with vigour. "You don't concentrate on what you're doing, Pippa. You never did.
What are you going to do while I see the district
officer and the schoolmaster?"

"I don't know," Pippa admitted.

"You see what I mean!" Mrs. Walker exclaimed
to Joel. "You'd think she'd be glad of the opportunity to do some work on her book, but I don't
suppose she will. She'll wander about, looking at
nothing at all, and then she'll wonder why she's
got nothing done!"

"It sounds a good idea to me," Joel answered
her. "May I come with you, Pippa?"

"You know the island," she objected. "You
don't have to bother with me. I can look round by
myself."

"I want to show you the island," he said.

"I haven't seen your house properly yet."

"Then we'll begin right here. The house is
traditional for this part of the world. Outsiders
think the women's apartments are screened and

hidden away to show their subjection to their menfolk, but it isn't really like that. In the Moslem world the houses belong to the women. They do all their entertaining there and order their household with as much severity as many a fabled potentate. The men live outside, coming home only to sleep and to be bossed about by their wives and mothers. I know many men who are afraid to go home to their poor downtrodden womenfolk!"

Pippa laughed. She turned eagerly to her mother. "Like Penelope! Do you remember, Mother? When her father didn't want her to marry, she lowered her veil to cover her face, thus showing her independence, and went off with her intended just the same."

Mrs. Walker laughed also. "I think you'd have trouble persuading most people that the veil is the symbol of Women's Liberation these days," she said, "but it was certainly how it began."

Having resolved that point to their mutual satisfaction, mother and daughter felt friendlier towards each other than they had for many a year. Pippa, who had never thought of herself as having much in common with either of her parents, wondered if it were more that she had never known either of them at all well.

Joel looked from one to the other of them with some amusement. "I'll go and see what's happened to lunch while you two rearrange history to suit yourselves—"

Lunch was an unexpectedly formal affair. The table was huge, practically filling the long, ornate room that Joel had turned into a dining room. Four or five servants, all clad in long white robes and coloured, highly embroidered, sleeveless jackets, stood behind each of the three placings, ready to serve the meal. They had placed Joel at one end, Mrs. Walker at the other and Pippa at the exact half-way mark. She was glad that no one was going to ask her to pass things back and forth, for she couldn't reach either of the others easily and would have been constantly on her feet, with no time to eat at all.

An enormous bowl of rice was brought round, followed by the main dish of the curry and so many side-dishes that Pippa soon lost count.

"What will you have to drink?" Joel asked the two women.

They both chose a homemade lemonade which was tart and refreshing on the tongue.

"I always enjoy eating in your house," Mrs. Walker remarked, smiling. "If you ever marry, you must keep your wife out of the kitchen. She'll only ruin things if she interferes with your cook."

Joel lifted an eyebrow, glancing thoughtfully at Pippa. "Did you do much cooking while you were married?" he asked her.

"Some," she answered reluctantly.

Her mother shrugged an impatient shoulder. "You couldn't boil an egg before your marriage!"

"I never had the opportunity to try," Pippa pointed out. "It doesn't take a genius to learn a few basic recipes however. Timothy—"

"The least said about Timothy the better!" her mother exclaimed.

Pippa addressed her food, her eyes misted with tears. "You never gave Timothy a chance. He knew what you all thought of him. It only made him worse."

"My dear, what else were we to think? Anyone could have seen what he was like!"

Pippa held her head high. "No one knew what he was like!" She shivered inwardly as her eyes met Joel's.

A muscle quirked in Joel's cheek and his eyes hardened. "I never liked him," he ground out, "but I can feel sorry for the chap. He had his problems, and Pippa is the last person he should have chosen to solve them for him!"

"Pippa chose him," Mrs. Walker drawled. "Marriage wasn't at all what he had in mind."

Pippa shut her eyes, but nothing could close her ears to Joel's crack of knowing laughter.

"What did he have in mind?"

Only Mrs. Walker had an answer to that. "Isn't it obvious? Pippa was a fool to encourage him, ruining her life like that. It won't be as easy for her to marry again as long as people remember who her first husband was. And what else is she going to do? She'll write this book—maybe—and then what?"

"I've told you, Mother—" Pippa began.

"Marriage isn't the only thing in life," Joel pointed out. "Maybe she'll surprise you by setting up house with a man who wants her as something more than a meal ticket. What d'you say, Pippa? Do you think you can handle both a man and a career of your own, as your mother did?"

Was he getting at her or her mother? "It

depends on the man—and the career. Would you like your wife to earn her own bread?"

"My wife, no."

Pippa shook her head at him. "Why not?"

His smile was very masculine and intimate, bringing the colour racing into her cheeks. "I shan't marry unless I find a woman I want with me night and day. Of course, if she were in your line of business, I daresay she could manage the occasional article."

"One has to learn to compromise in marriage," Pippa's mother said. "Joe and I nearly came unstuck at one time. In our day the wife was the one who had to give up everything for her husband, and so, naturally, that's what Joe expected me to do. I couldn't. It may be, Joel, that your wife won't be able to either." She glanced at her watch for the umpteenth time since their arrival. "I must go! No, I don't want any pudding, thank you. You know I never eat them. You'll be all right on your own, Pippa, won't you?"

Joel rose to his feet. "Pippa won't be alone."

Mrs. Walker looked surprised. "Oh, well, that's between the two of you," she said. "I'll be back sometime this evening."

Once again it was Joel who spoke. "Don't hurry. We'll wait dinner for you."

Mrs. Walker nodded, favouring her daughter with a keen glance that left Pippa feeling like a specimen under a microscope. She waited until her mother had gone and then she turned on Joel.

"You've no right to make her think that you—I —that there's anything between us!"

"Did I do that?"

"You did your best to make her think so!"

Joel looked amused. "It was you who did that, my sweet Pippa, blushing like a young girl when I talked about wanting my wife to be with me night and day. If anyone put any ideas into her head, it was you, not me."

Pippa glared at him.

Joel turned his whole attention onto choosing a bit of cheese from the tray that was being held out to him. Cheeses in Kenya were excellent, and almost all the different kinds were represented on the board. Joel kept a very good table, Pippa noted glumly. Marriage certainly wouldn't bring him any of the extra comforts of the usual kind. He could manage very well by himself, better than she could, so why should he bother? There had to be many women who were only too willing to share his bed.

Joel placed a piece of Stilton cheese on a biscuit and offered it to her. "It wasn't too bad with your mother, was it?"

"N-no. She still hates Timothy of course, but I think she's forgiven me. She brought me here with her, at any rate. She's always busy and I didn't hope for any more. One always had to settle for the bits of her that were left over from her work. I don't think either Daddy or I ever came first with her."

"Your father did."

Pippa frowned. Such a semi-detached marriage wouldn't do for her, she thought, any more than it would for Joel. She shrugged her shoulders. "Maybe. At least she has her work to keep her going now."

Joel offered her another piece of cheese. "What are you going to do this afternoon?"

"I'd like to see your house. I've never seen one quite like it before."

"The harem quarters?"

"All of it," she insisted.

He smiled slowly, watching her closely as she swallowed the bit of cheese and biscuit he had given her.

"We'll start with the women's quarters. They have a romantic quality that'll appeal to you. Was it only your mother you came to see, Pippa?"

The pulse hammered in her throat. "I didn't know you were here. I thought you were at Tsavo."

"Would you have come if you had known?"

She looked away, determined not to let him see how much his presence affected her. "Why not?" she said at last.

"You know why! When I'm close to you I can't keep my hands off you. Is that why you came?"

"Could be," she mocked him.

"I can't let you go again!"

"Nobody asked you to. It was your idea that I should go away and think about it, not mine."

He sighed heavily. "Heavens, Pippa, do you imagine that was the way I wanted it to be? That poor sucker you married didn't teach you a thing about men, did he? You're a walking temptation that I'm not even going to try to resist much longer! I want to take you upstairs and make love to you now. What do *you* want, Pippa?"

Pippa looked at him lovingly through her lashes. "I want to see your house," she reminded

him, a thread of laughter running through her
voice. "If you want to show it to me, that is."

He held out his hand to her and she put her
own into it, loving the warm feel of his skin
against hers.

Upstairs, in the harem area, Joel pushed back
the shutters to let in the strong sunlight.

"Well, what do you think?"

The rooms were very beautiful. Pippa exam-
ined the hand-made catches to the casements,
making the most of the moment. How many
women had lived in this house? She flickered a
glance in Joel's direction, turning her head a little
to take in the rest of the room. There were tiles on
the sides of the walls, imported probably from
North Africa, or across the sea from Aden. There
was a smell of sandalwood too, impregnated in
the sparse, heavy timbers of the ceiling. Much of
the room was magnificent, decorated with great
swirls of plaster work in which the dust had
settled, accentuating some of the more intricate
arabesques. Contrasting with this was a general
air of neglect where one of the walls was crum-
bling and another was badly cracked and in need
of repair.

Pippa answered Joel's question with one of her
own. "Have you lived here long?"

Joel smiled wryly. "I bought the house some
years ago, but I seldom get to spend more than a
couple of weeks here at a time."

"It doesn't look as though you've ever used
these rooms."

"Not often."

Something very like jealousy stirred within Pippa. "I suppose you keep your own harem here when you're in residence?" Her voice was light, but she couldn't entirely hide the anxiety behind the question.

"Would you care?"

"Of course not!" Pippa flashed her eyes at him. "What you do is nothing to do with me!"

"It could be." His body looked relaxed as he stood beside the window, staring out into the glare of the whitewashed street below. But she felt he was as aware of her as she was of him.

She moved away from the window, unable to bear the tension between them and seeking some way, any way, to relieve it. She didn't feel quite in control of her legs, but she forced them to carry her over to the bed, which was littered with cushions. She sat down on the edge, leaning back on her hands, her head thrown back.

He sat down on the bed beside her, pushing her back against the cushions with a gentle hand. "You're very beautiful, my Pippa," he whispered in her ear.

Her heart knocked against her ribs as she reached out to him and held him closer to her, easing his jacket over his shoulders and onto the floor.

He looked down at her for a long moment, his eyes dark with desire, then his mouth was moving against hers, teasing her lips apart. Pippa shut her eyes tight, burying her fingers in his hair, giving herself up to the delights of the moment with a freedom she had never experienced before. His arms were like bands of steel about her, the weight of his body preventing her from moving against him as she longed to do. With a murmur of protest, she pushed her hands up under his shirt, running her fingers along the flexed, powerful muscles of his back.

He drew back then, a smile tugging at the corner of his lips. "You have the advantage of me, Pippa darling. How do I get you out of this dress?"

She showed him the fastenings, helping him to drag it up over her head to join his jacket on the floor. She had very little on underneath, nothing to cushion the shock of his touch on her naked breasts. She would have uttered a protest if his mouth hadn't taken possession of hers again, and then it was too late; his hands were everywhere and she no longer wanted to stop him. On the contrary, she wanted him to go on and on and . . .

The footsteps were muffled but quite distinct, pausing only at the entrance to the room they were in. Pippa saw a black shadow in the doorway and her eyes opened wide with fright.

"What is it?" Joel demanded.

"There's someone there!"

For an instant Joel didn't move. Then he slowly turned away from her, rolling over to see what it was that had startled her.

"*Nani?*" he barked out.

An elderly woman, almost completely hidden by her black *bui-bui*, came slowly into the room. She looked at Pippa with open hostility, choosing to answer in English.

"I came to see if you wanted my daughter to

visit you tonight, but I see you've found somebody else. Shall I tell Tumi to wait until next
week?''

Joel swore beneath his breath. He levered
himself off the bed without a backward look at
Pippa. She lay back, the hurt that had been dealt
her almost overwhelming her. When she opened
her eyes again, the old woman and Joel were in
the corridor outside having a heated conversation
in highly idiomatic Swahili.

Pippa was fully dressed when Joel came back to
her. Even though his anger was not directed
towards her, she shivered at its impact, turning
away from the hot look in his eyes.

"I'm sorry to have made you change your
plans," she said evenly. "I hope you told her I'm
not staying. She came just in time, didn't she, to
stop us both from making fools of ourselves—"

"Pippa—"

She swayed where she stood. "Please don't
apologise! You were right! I didn't know what I
was doing. I thought—I hoped—I was someone
special to you." She hesitated, chewing on her
lower lip. "I didn't learn much from my marriage,
did I?"

"Pippa! Tumi hasn't been to this house for
weeks, nor has any other woman! She wouldn't
have been here in the first place if you hadn't
been married to someone else when we met in
Nairobi."

Pippa didn't believe a word he said. All she
knew was that Timothy had been right and that
no man would ever want her for herself. Joel had
been kind enough to pretend for a while, but he

would have gone back to Tumi sooner or later, as soon as he'd discovered that Pippa hadn't got what it took to keep a man interested in her. All in all, she had had a lucky escape.

"It doesn't matter. I'm sorry I misunderstood," she jerked out. And she ran out of the room as fast as she could in case he saw that she was crying. She was consumed by jealousy for the unknown Tumi.

She wiped the tears from her face with the back of her hands. Life was so unfair. Why did she have to be head over heels in love with a man who cared nothing about her?

Chapter Nine

She didn't want to see him ever again! She had thought she was special to him, as he had always been to her, not a passing fancy, a fool who had enticed him into a brief affair, no better and no worse than the half-dozen other women he had at his disposal.

"Pippa!"

She pretended not to hear him. Surely, he wouldn't dare come and find her in her bedroom. She sat on the chair in the corner, hugging herself for comfort, half-hoping he would come and half-hoping he wouldn't.

He came all right. He knocked briefly on the door and tried the door handle, only to discover that she had locked the door.

"Open up, Pippa!"

"No!"

"I want to speak to you!"

"Well, I don't want to speak to you! I don't want to see you! I don't want anything from you!"

Joel swore under his breath. "My love, don't you think you're being a trifle silly? I only want to talk."

"There's nothing to talk about!"

"Oh, isn't there?"

She read the determination in his voice rightly, but she trusted to the strength of the door and that he would soon give up.

She was wrong on both counts. The door splintered and gave way and Joel, grim of visage, stood in the doorway, rubbing his bruised shoulder.

"Don't ever lock the door against me again!" he shouted at her.

She was as angry as he. "How dare you come after me like this? You don't need me! You have Tumi—and how many others? Just because this is your house you needn't think you can browbeat me into doing something I don't want. I don't like crowds—"

Joel grasped her by the shoulders and shook her. Pippa gasped at the indignity, but she was afraid too. She had never seen him as angry as he was now. His eyes were two slits of darkness and his mouth was twisted into an ugly line that showed no signs of relenting, whatever she said.

"I'm beginning to think Timothy had a point! Listen to me, Pippa! You've got it all wrong! Tumi isn't my lover—"

Pippa sniffed. "You must think I'm a fool," she snapped back.

"I do!"

"Then why try to tell me a pack of lies that nobody in their right mind would ever think of believing?"

"I'm telling you the truth—if you'd only listen for a moment."

"I don't want to listen!"

"Tumi's got nothing to do with how we feel about each other. She's just an excuse, because you're scared of your own emotions. I wasn't going to do anything you didn't like, though, Pippa. Why make such a fuss because that old woman's timing was off?"

Pippa averted her gaze. "I don't want to talk about it any more," she declared. "I made a mistake, let's leave it at that. I—I thought you cared about me—*me* as a person. It seems to me that men never care about anybody except themselves. I can wait until I find someone who likes me as a person and not as a body to spend time with and then push out of the way—"

"Tumi is my cook's daughter—"

"I don't care who she is!"

Joel sighed, looking suddenly weary and defeated. "That's that then? You've got a lot of growing up to do yet, Pippa, before you'll find a man who suits your whims. I don't envy him, either, if you go on thinking of what you want and need, without a thought for his feelings. You'd better go back to Nairobi and write your book."

He was gone before she'd pulled herself together sufficiently to make any reply. She forgot her own part in the quarrel, hearing only his last, angry words to her. He'd told her to go away. The rejection was almost too hard to bear. Slowly, she crumpled and the tears began to come, silently pouring down her face, as the full force of the pain he had inflicted hit her. He may have been speaking the truth when he said Tumi was his cook's daughter, but it was easy to see what she was to Joel. She hadn't been mistaken in that. It would have been hard to have drawn any other conclusion from the old woman's words, or from Joel's first explanation of why the girl had visited him in the past. She knew she had been right, so why did Joel blame her for running out of the room in the harem? What had he expected her to do?

It was a long time before she had recovered sufficiently to change her clothes and set out to find her mother. It wasn't going to be easy to tell her that she was going back to Nairobi without even spending one night in Lamu. Her mother would guess that Joel was at the bottom of her sudden retreat, and Pippa couldn't see her taking her daughter's part in any quarrel between them. She admired Joel and she wouldn't believe he could be anything less than perfect, whereas she'd never had much time for Pippa and, after Timothy, she was even less likely to take her daughter's part in anything.

Pippa packed the few things she had brought with her and, taking them with her, crept downstairs and out of the house. Half an hour had done more than transform her whole life; it seemed as if the whole world was prepared to weep in sympathy. Thunder rumbled overhead as great black clouds veiled the sun and threatened to turn dusty streets into puddles of running mud. Even the breeze from the sea had died away, making it hotter and stickier than ever. It was uncomfortable work, lugging her bags as she made her way towards the waterfront where she hoped to catch sight of her mother.

She had never been alone in such an area before. At first she found it interesting, watching an ocean-going dhow, or Boom, unloading its cargo at the wharf. Pippa thought the captain looked a thorough-going villain and his crew very little better. Most of them wore no more than loin-cloths, hitched up between their legs and knotted to one side. Their bare bodies shone with sweat as they unloaded their valuable cargo of salt and carpets and loaded up again with the tough mangrove poles that were so much in demand in Arabia for building purposes, as they were resistant to the ravages of the white ant.

Beyond the Boom were the smaller coastal dhows, which plied their trade between Mombasa and Lamu. They made a fantastic picture of swaying masts against the leaden sky of the approaching rain.

A woman in a *bui-bui* came slowly up the street towards her, pausing to look into the dim, cool stores of the carpet-sellers, the goldsmiths, wood-carvers, tailors, and the low-ceilinged coffee houses, all of them made mysterious by the overhanging balconies that almost met overhead across the narrow streets.

The woman looked familiar, though perhaps that wasn't surprising, as all the women, shrouded as they were in black, looked very much the same as they wandered up and down the narrow streets. Nowadays, few of them veiled their faces as a gesture to modern times, but they were adept at moving into the shadows and masking their features by the careful way they held their heads, drawing their head-covering forwards at the same time. Occasionally one would catch glimpses of the silks and satins and the gold and silver jewellery many of them wore underneath, but it was rude to stare at any woman outside her own house. Good manners made one pretend these black bundles of washing didn't exist. If one looked at them at all, one looked right through them as if they were invisible and of no interest to anyone.

As the woman drew closer, Pippa recognised her as Tumi's mother, and she turned her back on her, dismayed by the agonising pain that had her heart in its grip every time she thought of Joel's mistress. Was she pretty? Some of the young, half-Arab women Pippa had seen had a loveliness that would have stirred any painter to get out his paints, if capturing the image of any living being had been acceptable to any of the strict, orthodox Moslems that made up the citizenry of Lamu and most of the coastal area of Kenya.

"*Memsahib*, what you doing alone here?" the old woman accosted her. Her eyes glittered with malice.

"I'm looking for my mother," Pippa told her.

She looked at her more closely, fascinated by the ring she wore in her nose, never having seen one quite like it before. She made a gesture towards her nose-piece. "I've never seen one like it." Pippa explained her rudeness.

"The Bajun traditionally wear such pieces."

"Does your daughter?"

The woman shrugged. "Her father is not Bajun. He came across the seas from another land. Bwana Buchanan says my daughter is the most beautiful girl in the islands. He pays her good money."

"I'm sure he does," Pippa said dryly.

"If you stay, he won't want her. None of the white men who have their own women with them—"

"I'm not staying! That's why I'm looking for my mother. I want to tell her that I'm going back to Nairobi now, tonight if I can get there."

A bony finger poked her in the ribs. "It's good you go. You don't belong here on the islands."

"Why not?" Pippa asked her curiously.

"White women get ill and die."

"My mother seems to manage," Pippa pointed out.

"*Memsahib* Walker is not like other white women. She speaks as one of us and listens to Tumi as the old men do." The woman spat with deadly accuracy into the gutter. "You are afraid all the time you're here. You're afraid of everything you see!"

Pippa couldn't deny it. The thing she was most afraid of, however, was of getting lost in the maze of narrow streets. The people interested her more than they frightened her. Besides, she had known people very like them all her life because they were the people her mother worked amongst. She had heard their myths and children's stories long before she had been told any of the usual tales other white children were told at their mother's knee.

"I may never have been here before, but I bet I could tell you a thing or two about these islands," she claimed.

The old woman gave her a look of pure contempt. "You can tell me nothing."

"My mother——" Pippa began. It wasn't often she had occasion to boast of her mother being a leading authority on the remains of the ancient coastal culture known as Swahilini, but she thought herself justified in doing so now.

"——is not you!" the old woman cut her off.

"Nevertheless, I've heard stories of Lamu, Manda, Pate and the others all my life."

"And you're still afraid to be found alone in our streets?"

"I was looking for my mother."

"So you said, but she isn't free to speak to you now. You'll have to wait for her if you want to see her before this evening. Come, you may come and wait in my house if you like. There are no men there to stare at you and make you wonder if they mean to carry you off to the harem of some rich Arab in Arabia!"

"In these days?" Pippa scoffed.

"Isn't that what you're afraid of? Men?"

"Of course not!"

But it wasn't entirely true. She wasn't afraid, but she was cautious of being hurt again as Timothy had hurt her. Perhaps she had made too much of Joel's relationship with Tumi? If she had loved him less, she might have accepted other women in his life, but her love was still so new and all-consuming that the thought of his making love to any other woman tore her apart. She would be better away from him, rather than settling for a compromise that would bring her nothing but misery all her life long.

It was probably foolish of her to go with the old woman, but she went just the same, following the graceful black-covered woman down half-a-dozen identical streets, peering into the small dark shops as she went. Everywhere, the same words of welcome greeted her ears: *"Jambo, habari, salaam alaikum."* She noticed that the further they went from the tourist area the less they used the more formal *memsahib* and reverted to the African *mama*, a word of respect for every married woman, or an unmarried one of a certain age, though there were mighty few of those within the African culture.

She answered the greetings as was appropriate, modestly turning her back as she did so and never, never looking straight into the face of the artisan who was trying to sell his wares to her.

At last they came to a stop by a tiny house and she was taken upstairs to a small, narrow room, furnished with only a couple of wooden chairs.

"My son will fetch you something to drink," the old woman told her, seating herself comfortably on her feet on the floor and nodding towards one of the chairs.

Pippa knew better than to refuse, though the thought of having to cope with a fizzy, sweet drink out of a cup that was probably less than clean revolted her. She had underrated her hostess, however, for the cup that was brought to her was hand-made, of beaten silver, and the coffee was hot and freshly made, just as it had been served in Joel's house.

"Does Tumi live with you here, too?" Pippa asked politely.

"Until she marries."

"Where is she now?" Pippa forced herself to ask. The last thing she wanted was to see her rival, but she couldn't help being curious about her.

"There are white men come to see her," the old woman said with pride. "One of them has come from England and another from even further away. These days, a girl may make as much use of her schooling as any boy. Of all my children, Tumi will make our old age secure with what she earns. My husband says it's all wrong for a girl to meet men in the same room as she does, but he admits the money is good. She can earn in a day what he will earn in a whole month."

When Pippa had finished her coffee, the old woman rose to her feet with the natural grace of her race and beckoned for Pippa to follow her.

"Your mother will be finished now. Come, I'll take you to her."

Pippa would have liked to have asked her how she knew so much about her mother's move-ments, but there was no opportunity as the old woman hugged her *bui-bui* closer about her, her dark eyes flashing as she summoned her son to clear away the used coffee cups. It seemed she treated everyone with the same gruff way of speaking and the same contemptuous look of dislike. Perhaps it was no more than the set of her features, with her wide, flaring nostrils and the slight frown just above the bridge of her nose.

The streets were as busy as ever as they hurried along them. They throbbed with activity: a fisherman carrying a string of huge, silver fish; a small boy hurrying through the crowds with a silver tray laden with tiny cups of amber liquid, the sweet tea which was such a favourite drink of the artisans as they worked.

"How do you know where my mother is?" Pippa asked, when she at last recognised one of the mosques they were passing.

The old woman shrugged, showing her teeth in a sudden smile. "We all know your mother. She was here all the time when she was working on the island of Ishakani. She would tell us about the coral stone houses there, all lying in ruins, and the strange places of worship the like of which she'd never seen before. She is a great teacher! It's a pity you don't listen to her! Young people are all the same these days; none of them ever want to listen to their parents!"

"I won't believe your children don't listen to you!" Pippa exclaimed.

"I make sure they do! Your mother has no time to run after you all day long. Why should she, with you being a married woman?"

"A widow."

The old woman laughed. "A bit of a girl like you? Tell that to Bwana Buchanan!"

"I have," Pippa told her.

The woman chuckled, her whole body shaking with mirth. "What did he say to that? My, my, no wonder he makes you so welcome in his house. Does your mother know about that, I wonder?"

"It's none of her business," Pippa said stiffly.

The woman shook her head. "White people have strange ways. They wouldn't do for my people."

She led the way down the last of the streets and pointed towards the offices of the district officer. "There you are! You'll find your mother there by now."

Pippa tried to thank her for her hospitality, but the old woman dismissed her gratitude as if she were swatting an irritating fly. "You take heed now of what your mother tells you! You hear me?"

Pippa twisted her lips into a smile. If her mother noticed she were there at all, it was unlikely she would bother to offer her any advice as to what she should do next.

"I hear you." She shook hands the African way, with an exchanged grasping of the thumbs, and stood there for a long moment, watching the old woman walk away from her down the street. Impossible as it seemed, she had actually liked her, despite her being Tumi's mother.

A breeze rose as suddenly as it had died earlier, and a frond of palm leaves scraped against the wall beside her, recalling her to what she was doing there. She turned away and walked slowly across the road to the offices, pushing open the door and going inside.

Her mother looked up, surprise on her face.
"What are you doing here? Is Joel with you?"

Pippa shook her head. "I came to find you. I'm
going back to Nairobi."

She thought her mother looked tired and hot,
but, although she looked for it, she couldn't
detect a glimmer of emotion over her daughter's
unexpected decision.

"Oh? Well, while you're here you'd better
meet the district officer. He's just about to show
me the famous side-blown horns, or *siwas*, of the
islands. They may interest you too."

Pippa couldn't have been less interested. She
wanted to talk about Joel, though heaven only
knew what she would find to tell her mother
about him. There was really nothing to say,
except that she wanted him so badly she thought
she'd go mad with the longing. Her mother might
even think she was being silly to mind about
Tumi. Anyway, it wasn't the sort of thing she felt
she could discuss with her. They'd never been on
those terms, and the last thing she wanted was to
embarrass her mother.

The district officer came back into the office,
the sweat pouring down his face in large drops
that he brushed away on the sleeve of his immacu-
late tropical suit. Pippa wondered that he didn't
wear the long, cool robes most of the other men
favoured in Lamu. He was undoubtedly a Moslem like them, probably brought up amongst
them, but the British traditions in government
died hard.

Mrs. Walker came alive when she saw the

siwas. "Aren't these magnificent? And quite two
hundred years old. Look at the craftsmanship!"

Pippa hadn't been listening. "Mother, if I don't
leave now I'll never get to Nairobi tonight!" she
said impatiently.

"Why d'you want to go? I thought you and Joel
were getting along famously."

"He asked me to go," Pippa told her.

"Joel did?" Her mother hesitated, as if she
were on the point of saying something more.
"Oh, very well, I'll come and see you off. What
will you do? Get a room in a hotel?"

"For tonight. Tomorrow I may go looking for
an apartment of my own. I can't afford hotels for
long."

Her mother nodded. "Try and get a room in
Muthaiga. Your father and I used to have a place
there near the forest."

"I'll try."

There didn't seem to be anything to say after
that. The district officer shook hands with Pippa
and, rather more enthusiastically, with her mother, beseeching the older woman to come and see
him any time she thought he could be of use to
her. It was obvious he thought as highly of her as
did Tumi's mother.

"There's no need for you to come," Pippa said
aloud. "I only came to say goodbye."

"Of course I'll see you off! Spend the night at
my place in Malindi and go on to Nairobi in the
morning. Have you all your things? Good, then
we needn't go back to the house for anything.
Every step counts when there's no breeze!"

"I'd rather go straight to Nairobi," Pippa argued with her.

"I daresay, but I don't think of you wandering round Africa in the middle of the night by yourself! I suppose Joel didn't offer to go with you?"

"No, Mother, he didn't."

Mrs. Walker smiled an ironical smile. "Bad luck! Come on, let's go."

They were only just in time for Pippa to catch the ferry over to the mainland. She made her way through the goats and people to a vacant seat and sat down on it quickly. The last she saw of Lamu was her mother standing on the wharf, waving a coloured handkerchief over her head, just as she'd waved her goodbye when she'd been going back to school as a child. In some ways nothing changed, Pippa thought sadly.

Chapter Ten

Normally Pippa felt a lift to her spirits whenever she arrived in Nairobi. Of all the cities she had ever been to this was the one she loved the best. She loved the contrasts between the first colonial buildings and the new, ultra-modern ones that dominated the skyline. There were buildings like the circular, 440-foot-high Conference Centre, where thousands of delegates could be seated in the vast session hall, panelled in olive-wood; the Hilton Hotel; the new government buildings; and the jumble of cathedrals, mosques and Hindu temples that accentuated the cosmopolitan character of Nairobi life.

The misery, seated somewhere in her chest, refused to go away. She may have decided to have nothing more to do with Joel, but half her being had been left behind in Lamu and she didn't think she'd ever be the same again. Almost, she could have turned tail and run back to him. Indeed, it was only her pride that kept her mooching about the city, filling in time she could ill afford to waste if she ever was to find herself the accommodation she needed, let alone work on the biography of her father.

It was inevitable that she should drift towards the Thorn Tree, the street café outside the New Stanley Hotel where she had first met Joel and had first felt the full force of the attraction he would have for her until she died. She didn't want to go there, nor did she want to seat herself at one of the tables under the thorn tree that had long since replaced the original one from which the café had acquired its name.

She was near enough the tree to see the notice board it carried on the lower part of its trunk. Once, when Kenya had been young, the white hunters had pinned their messages for each other and their clients directly onto the yellow-green trunk. The custom had been continued, though most of the messages these days were either banal or facetious, such as "Lift wanted to Cairo. Will share driving," or the even more common one of simply stating that one had been there on such and such a day at such and such a time.

Pippa's surprise was therefore overwhelming when she caught a glimpse of her own name neatly printed on the side of the board that was facing where she was sitting:

PIPPA GREGSON, NÉE WALKER: PLEASE
TELEPHONE ROSAMUND MASSEK BEFORE
DOING ANYTHING ELSE.

She had never heard of Rosamund Massek.

She studied the message for a long moment,
barely noticing that her Tusker beer had been
brought to her and that the waiter was awaiting
payment. Whoever Rosamund Massek was, she
must have been pretty desperate to have pinned
up a message for Pippa. Perhaps Rosamund Massek had heard that Pippa was working on a
biography of her father. Why else would she want
to get in touch?

Pippa downed the cold beer, half wishing she
had ordered a coffee instead. After the turgid
heat of the coast, the sparkling air of Nairobi felt
cool against her skin. Getting to her feet, she
smiled at the young couple who were eagerly
seating themselves at her vacated table. It was
obvious they were part of a party of Europeans,
who came in droves to spend a week seeing the
animals and then another week sunning themselves on the silver beaches, quite unaware that
the heat of the sun at the Equator was quite
different from anything they had experienced
back home.

The New Stanley Hotel produced a telephone
book and she looked hastily down the M's for the
name of Massek. There was a Geoffrey Massek
with a Nairobi number and she wrote it down on
the piece of paper the receptionist offered her. It
was impossible to tell where the Masseks lived

because all the addresses were given with post office box numbers, just as they had been fifty years before when everyone had collected their mail from the centre of town.

The number rang a few times and then a female voice answered.

"This is Pippa Gregson—"

"At last! I've been searching the whole of Nairobi for you! Look, I can't explain on the phone. Could you come over to our house for lunch, say, in an hour's time?"

"I could," Pippa agreed cautiously. "I don't know where you live, however."

"Muthaiga. Right at the end of Naivasha Avenue. You can't miss it!"

Pippa had heard that before. "What's it all about?"

"Oh lord, don't you know who I am?"

"No." Then more curiously, "Should I?"

"I suppose not. I just thought you would, seeing how we know all about you. I'm Joel's sister."

"I didn't know he had one," Pippa said dully.

Surprisingly, Rosamund laughed. "He has a family. Did you think he was hatched out of a chrystal egg, as the Africans used to think was the way of white folk?"

"I hadn't thought about it," Pippa responded, nettled.

"Then you won't know that this is his house," his sister continued. "Geoffrey and I are supposed to be having him to stay with us, though we haven't seen hide nor hair of him so far. First of

all, he was chasing elephants in your company
and then he shot down to the coast, muttering
he'd be back as soon as he could get here—"

"He's staying at his house on Lamu, if that's
what you want to know. My mother's with him."

"Well, that's something to know. Okay, my
dear, we'll expect you as soon as you can get here.
'Bye for now."

Pippa replaced the receiver feeling colder than
ever. She stood in front of the telephone, wondering if she dared ring back and say she wasn't going
to lunch after all. If all Rosamund wanted to
know was where her brother was, she didn't have
to spend hours in her company for that! She
didn't want to have anything more to do with Joel
Buchanan, or his sister either. The sooner she
forgot all about him, the sooner she could get on
with making a life of her own, she thought
unhappily.

The New Stanley was only too pleased that she
should use one of their rooms to change her dress
and smart up her appearance for lunch.

"We're sorry we can't offer you a room for the
night," the receptionist apologised. "We have so
many package tours passing through these days,
and quite a few of them like to place their people
with us. We're part of the old life and, I must say,
I hope we never change."

"So do I," Pippa agreed.

From the few things she had with her, she
selected one of the new dresses that looked like a
blouse and skirt, which she had bought in London. It had a cherry-red pleated skirt, a chrystal
pleated sleeveless jacket and a cream-colored top,

embroidered in the same red as the rest of the outfit. In London it had seemed cool and decidedly smart. Now for the first time that day she felt warm and she hoped she would not be too hot by the time she got herself to Muthaiga and the unknown Rosamund Massek.

It seemed no time at all before the taxi had whisked her out of the city proper and into the tree-lined suburb, with the jacarandas at their very best, each of them standing in a pool of mauve blossom recently fallen from the abundance that still covered their branches. Here and there was a splodge of bougainvillea, much of it in the new exotic colours that covered the whole spectrum from pink to orange to the bright purple for which it was originally famous.

The Masseks' drive dipped down towards a grey-stone house set in a colourful garden, the lawn of which the gardener was mowing in a desultory manner, a battered straw hat set right on the back of his head at such a jaunty angle that Pippa wondered how he kept it on.

She paid off the taxi and walked down the few steps to the open front door. The house smelt of polished hard wood and the scent of flowers that someone had arranged with abandon on every available surface. It was a welcoming house, Pippa thought with appreciation, as she looked about her.

"Hodi!" she called out.

Her hostess came herself to greet her. Pippa would have recognised her anywhere. She had Joel's light hair, the same firm features, softened only slightly by her gender, and the same way of moving, as though she knew exactly where she was going.

"My dear, how good of you to come! I've sent Geoffrey to the Club for lunch because he keeps saying that Joel will be furious if I interfere in his affairs, and he's probably right, which makes it all the more annoying, if you know what I mean. Joel isn't making a very good job of managing by himself, and what else is a sister for?" She blinked myopically at the shorter Pippa before enveloping her in an affectionate embrace. "How smart you are!" she commented. "Now that is one thing that I wasn't told about you."

"I bought this in London," Pippa found herself explaining. It was a completely inappropriate thing to say, she thought, because the clothes in Nairobi were every bit as *chic* as in any of the great centres of *haute couture* in Europe, providing one had the money to pay for them.

"Come and sit down," Rosamund invited her, leading the way up two steps into a vast sitting room with a roof like a church and a minstrels' gallery formed by the staircase rising from one end of the room. "What will you have to drink?"

Pippa chose a soft drink made from a mixture of citrus and passion fruit, a little amused by her hostess' hesitation before she poured herself the same, adding a cube of ice to both glasses.

"Cheers!" she murmured as she seated herself on the comfortable Sanderson-covered sofa.

Pippa responded in kind, taking a sip and immediately feeling much better for the tangy taste on her tongue.

"You don't smoke, do you?" Rosamund went on. "Joel said you didn't."

Pippa was startled. "Joel did?"

Her hostess looked unexpectedly nervous. "He's been talking about you for years," she said on a throwaway line. "He knew your father very well, of course. They were going to combine on a book, but I expect you know all about that." She looked more uncomfortable than ever. "Joel is a remarkably fine photographer. Perhaps you saw his exhibition in London last year?"

Pippa could hardly believe her ears. "I did nothing but work in London," she said defensively.

"And buy clothes?"

"That was a last-minute impulse. I thought a new me was necessary to the way I saw myself. I was an awful frump all the time I was married to Timothy."

"That's what you think!" Rosamund's eyes twinkled in a way that was very reminiscent of her brother. "I have it on the best authority that you were young and sweet and much in need of someone to look after you."

Pippa sighed. "Joel again?"

Rosamund nodded. "It was just as well he felt like that," she went on casually. "He could have made life very difficult for you if he hadn't. He could prove that Timothy stole your father's find. He'd already photographed the evidence before Timothy got there."

Pippa swallowed. "I suppose my father asked him to keep it quiet?"

"Well, I don't know all the ins and outs," Rosamund admitted, "but I've always understood that it was Joel who refused to have you put in the pillory for something Timothy had done. He was pretty bleak about it at the time."

And had only shown her kindness ever since! Pippa could have understood him better if he had gone ahead and published all that he knew. She blinked, thinking what a fool she had been to suppose it had been her father who had tried to protect her happiness. With both her parents it was the truth which came first, always. She could hear her father explaining now that happiness based on a lie would soon falter and fail anyway, so it was better to face facts at once and rebuild one's life on a surer foundation. She was pretty sure that Joel's instincts would have led him to the same conclusion, so why had he tried to protect her from Timothy's lie?

"I hardly knew Joel. I don't really know him now. My mother took me to Lamu with her. I didn't know she was staying in Joel's house there. Joel asked me to leave."

"*Joel* did?"

Pippa lifted her chin to combat the remembered pain. "He was having Tumi around that evening. I don't suppose you—"

"You should have stayed no matter what Joel said!" Rosamund exclaimed. "No, perhaps you shouldn't have done, not unless your Swahili is a great deal better than mine. Oh, I can manage here and up country, because we all speak the same kitchen variety, but it's different down at the Coast. Joel is the only one who understands all the nuances. Geoffrey is worse than I am."

Pippa maintained a discreet silence. She wouldn't have thought an intimate knowledge of Swahili would have been helpful either way; it was Joel's intimate knowledge of Tumi that she had objected to.

Rosamund swallowed down the last of her drink. "Lunch!" she announced. "I hope you're hungry. Our cook takes offence if everyone doesn't over-eat every time he goes to town on one of his creations. As soon as I told him you were coming, he insisted on doing one of Joel's favourites for you. *Katlesi ya ng'ombe.*"

"Beef fillet, covered with hashed brown potatoes," Pippa translated. "It's one of my favourites too."

"Mpishi will be pleased. I sometimes think he only agrees to work for me because I let him do as he likes. He's an elder of his tribe and terribly grand, whereas my only claim to fame is that I'm Joel's sister."

"Is that why he works for you?" Pippa teased her.

"Well, he's never actually said so," Rosamund acknowledged, "but he gets very down at the mouth if Joel doesn't appear at regular intervals. He's nearly driven me mad these last few days when Joel was expected but never came."

Pippa looked down her nose. "There's only Tumi to keep him on Lamu now," she said.

"No, there isn't!" Rosamund presented a crestfallen face, though she waited until they were settled at table before going on. "The thing is that when you told me where Joel is, I rang him up to ask if he would soon be here, and that Arab—at least I think he's an Arab—cook of his told me he's too ill to do anything at the moment. He's gone down with malaria and is feeling perfectly ghastly! If your mother hadn't been there, I'd have gone down myself to see him over the hump—"

"I'd hate to be nursed by my mother!"

"Why? She's a lovely person!"

"Yes, I know she is! She might even get the doctor if she noticed you were at death's door, but the chances are that she'd be far too involved in her own work to realise she hadn't seen you about for a day or so."

Rosamund laughed. "She is a bit like that," she agreed. "You must have had a lonely childhood. Is that why you married Timothy?"

Pippa nodded. "How did you guess?"

Rosamund shrugged. "There had to be some reason and it seemed the most likely. It's a pity you didn't meet Joel first."

"I don't suppose it'd have made any difference."

Her hostess looked at her with interest. "You're right, you don't know Joel very well. Don't worry—"

"But I do worry! If he's got malaria, it was all my fault! I forgot to take my tablets with me and he gave me his when we were camped by this water-hole." The tears rushed into her eyes. "I seem to bring him nothing but trouble!"

"The way he told it, he practically kidnapped

you to go running after his elephants with him," Rosamund remarked dryly.

"The Empress lost her temper with his aeroplane and walked all over it. The Landrover was the only transport we had left between us. I could hardly leave him stranded when it was my fault that he'd left his plane. He wanted to warn me the elephants were passing through, you see. They'd smelt the rain on the wind and nothing was going to stop them from moving south to find the water."

"You don't sound as if you minded too much?"

"No." Pippa bit her lip. "No, I didn't. I rather enjoyed it, as a matter of fact. I just wish I knew Joel was all right—"

"Why don't you go down and see?"

"He won't want to see me!"

"You think not? But, if your mother isn't going to nurse him, who else is going to? Geoffrey is counting on me being in Nairobi for the next few days, so I can't go. Malaria isn't the sort of thing one can shrug off by trying to look after oneself, you know. It's a killer even today."

"I've only just got back to Nairobi!" Pippa wailed. "I can't afford to keep flying back and forth. Supposing he tells me to go away again?"

"If I were you, I'd get in first and make sure he doesn't get the opportunity," his sister advised frankly. "Tell him from me, he'll only regret it and have to start running after you all over again, which would be a waste of time when you'd both obviously much rather be together—"

"There's still Tumi!"

Rosamund shrugged. "If you don't want her there, tell her to go away!"

"Her mother—"

Rosamund chuckled. "Is she still around? She's always thought she could come and go as she likes because her husband works for Joel. Tell *him* if you have any trouble! That'll spike her guns! She won't dare go against him, not on Lamu, where women are invisible beings and do as they're told!"

"Joel says they rule their own homes with rods of iron."

"But Joel's house isn't her home, or Tumi's, or any woman's. It could be yours, on the other hand, if you want to live out of a suitcase half your life and in that dreadful house for the other half—"

"Joel doesn't even like me!"

"My dear girl, Joel's been in love with you for years! What do you want him to do to prove it to you?"

Pippa opened her mouth and shut it again. "All right," she said at last, "I'll go back to Lamu until he's back on his feet, but I can't promise anything after that."

"Good enough," said Rosamund. "Excuse me a minute, and I'll get Geoffrey to put you on the next plane for Malindi. Can you manage from there?"

Pippa set her mouth in a firm line. "Of course I can," she said.

It was hotter than ever down at the Coast. A pewter sky brooded over a leaden sea while palm trees drooped over the silver sands, the little patches of shade they afforded occupied by the few tourists who had ventured out of the air-conditioned hotels of the main resorts.

The nearer she got to the Lamu boat, the more nervous Pippa became of the reception she would get from Joel. By the time she had seated herself on the ferry and they were pulling away from the mainland towards the island, she was almost hoping that Joel's malaria would be so bad that he wouldn't recognise her. She pictured herself nursing him selflessly back to health, making her exit as soon as the fever broke and she knew he was going to be all right. Somehow, though, she couldn't imagine Joel out of his mind and unable to cope with any situation that presented itself to him. If he told her to go away again . . .

Walking through the narrow streets of Lamu was like walking through waist-deep water. By the time Pippa reached Joel's house, her clothes were sticking to her flesh and her hair was as wet as if she had just finished washing it. If she had wanted to look attractive for Joel she might as well put it out of her mind, she reflected sourly. She looked and felt a wreck.

It was deliciously cool inside. She stood for a long moment, her eyes shut as she tried to regain her composure before she called out to let them know she was there. In the end, she didn't have to. Her mother, looking neat and well in control of herself and everything else, came down the stairs towards her, completely unsurprised to see her daughter back again.

"Where's Joel?" Pippa demanded.

Her mother lifted two perfectly formed eyebrows. "Have you lost him?"

"Mother, you know as well as I do he's in bed with fever! How is he?"

Mrs. Walker glanced at her watch. "You've caught me at a bad time, my dear. I'm afraid I'm just going out. Pity you weren't here last night. You missed a great treat! I'll tell you about it at dinner."

Pippa glowered at her. "Don't you care about Joel?"

Her mother walked purposefully through the hall, pecking her daughter on the cheek as she passed by.

"Should I?" she asked vaguely. "You seem to care enough for both of us, if you don't mind my saying so, dear."

"He wouldn't have malaria if he hadn't given me his pills!"

Mrs. Walker considered that statement. "I don't think that can be right, dear. Most people take one pill a month these days—I forget what they're called—and that does. In my opinion, the government ought to hand them out to the whole population. It couldn't cost as much as all that!"

"Less than one battleship to immunise the whole world."

Her mother's head jerked upwards, her interest caught. "How d'you know that?"

"Joel told me."

"Really? What a sinful world it is that they don't do it then. Oh well, I must be off! You're looking tired, dear. If I were you, I'd have a quick shower and a change of clothing before you go searching for Joel. By the way, how was Rosamund?"

"I liked her. I liked Geoffrey too, but I didn't see so much of him. How did you know I'd seen her?"

"How else would you know about Joel?" her mother countered with unanswerable logic and, putting up her parasol, she marched out of the door for all the world as if it were a spring day in England.

Pippa went slowly upstairs. She felt better after she'd had a shower and shampooed her hair. She wasn't even surprised when she quit the bathroom for her bedroom and came face to face with one of the prettiest girls she had ever seen in her life.

"Tumi?" she hazarded.

The girl nodded. "I came for my things. It was too late last night to take them home with me, but my father will help me carry them now."

"What things?" Pippa asked.

"My musical instruments, a Swahili oboe, and another one a bit like a guitar. I need them when I recite." The girl smiled suddenly. "I'm glad you came back! You'll find Joel up in the harem quarters, like a bear with a sore head—"

"One feels dreadful with malaria!" Pippa defended him quickly.

"And even worse when one's heart is hurting! I'll tell my father you're here for dinner, shall I? Goodbye for now!"

"Goodbye," said Pippa weakly. She watched the girl as she hurried across the landing and went down the stairs, her trousers under her skirt making a delicious feminine sound as she walked. At last it all fell into place: Tumi obviously entertained by reciting the lengthy Swahili epics on which her mother was so keen. No wonder white men came from afar to visit her! Most of the troubadours of Africa were men, even in these enlightened days.

The heat fell away from her as she brushed her hair into the prettiest style she could manage. And now for Joel, she thought with a mounting sense of excitement. Now for Joel and her heart's desire!

Chapter Eleven

The shadows of evening made the house dark and mysterious. In another few minutes it would be completely dark. There was no reason to be afraid of the strange atmosphere of the harem quarters, but it was hard to walk about them as if they had been any other rooms. It was almost as if the ghosts of the women who had inhabited them in earlier times were still as much present as the scent of sandalwood.

"Joel?"

It was meant to be a shout, but it came out as a whisper. He heard her all the same.

"You're back, are you?"

She whirled about, astonished as much by the firmness of his voice as by the fact that she hadn't noticed him lying on the bed where he had so nearly made love to her—was it only the day before yesterday?

"Do you mind?"

"It depends on why you're here."

She sank down onto the edge of the bed beside him, her knees unable to support her a minute longer. He pulled the loose sheets more closely about him in a defensive movement that was like a knife twisting in her heart.

"I was told you had malaria."

"So? Your mother was here. *Tumi* was here!"

"And Tumi's mother. Which one of them was going to nurse you better?"

A reluctant smile tugged at the corners of his mouth. "I'd say Tumi was the best bet, only I don't think her family would approve, somehow. I don't suppose she's ever been alone with a man in her whole life."

Pippa took a deep breath. "It would have been kinder if you'd told me that before," she rebuked him.

"You wouldn't have believed me," he said in matter-of-fact tones. "I'm surprised you believe me now."

She averted her face, taking advantage of the shadows to hide her expression from him.

"I'd still be here even if I didn't. What are you doing up here?"

"Thinking of the might-have-been."

She turned round to look at him properly. "Have you had malaria?" she accused him.

"A mild dose."

"Rosamund made it sound as if you were at death's door!"

"Ah!" He relaxed visibly. "How did she find you?"

"She put a notice up at the Thorn Tree Café asking me to telephone her. I stopped for the night at my mother's house in Malindi, so none of the hotels knew where I was."

"It sounds as though she went to a great deal of trouble to find you," he commented.

Pippa flicked a glance at him. "She had the odd idea that you wouldn't be able to manage without me."

"I wonder what gave her that impression," he drawled.

"It must have been something you said!"

He was silent for a long moment, then he shifted his position on the bed a few inches to give her more room and said, "It sounds to me that my sister has turned into a blabbermouth of the first order. What other delectable items did she let fall?"

For the first time for a long, long while Pippa felt as though she were in a position to take charge of her own life. "Nothing that I didn't know before," she said coolly, "or couldn't have guessed if I hadn't allowed you to blind me to the one thing that matters. I was in such a bother as to what you were thinking, I didn't give myself time to think at all! And you weren't much better!" She rounded on him. "How could you have been so stupid, and noble, and—and unlike yourself!"

He put out a hand and touched her cheek very gently. "Are you blushing, Pippa? Damn this darkness! Let's get the lamps lit—"

As if in answer to his command, a black-clad

figure came shuffling along the corridor outside
and knocked softly on the door.

"Is there anything you want, Bwana Joel, before I go home?"

"Come in, Mama."

Pippa froze where she was sitting as Tumi's
mother pushed open the door and came into the
room, a lighted hurricane-lamp swinging from
one hand.

"Shall I light the lamps, Bwana?"

Her eyes fell on Pippa and the frown between
her eyes became more pronounced than ever. "If
you're here, I'm going! There's nothing wrong
with you that you can't light the lamps, is there?"

"No," Pippa managed. She still wasn't sure if
Tumi's mother resented her presence in the
house, or if it was just her gruff manner that made
her seem so disapproving.

"Then I'll leave the matches."

She took them out of a pocket somewhere in
her robes and threw them accurately into Pippa's
lap.

"No need to ask you why you're here!" she
went on grumpily. "Ah well, you won't be need-
ing me, that's for sure. Does your mother know
you've come?"

Pippa nodded. "I met her on her way out.
She'll be back later—"

The old woman turned away, satisfied. "You
just behave yourselves till she gets back, you hear
me? Goodnight to the two of you."

"Salaams, Mama," Joel responded, amusement tugging at the corners of his mouth. He
waited until she had gone, and then he threw back

his head and laughed. "I wonder if I'll ever get you wholly to myself," he groaned.

Pippa busied herself with trimming the lamps, hoping he wouldn't notice how her hands were trembling.

"In Africa?" she mocked him.

"Why not in Africa?" he demanded. "The whole population can't be made up of goats and goatish old women!"

"And stupid, noble men," Pippa added.

"I suppose I deserved that," he acknowledged. "Come here, and I'll see if I can do better this time round."

She shook her head. "It's my turn," she claimed. A match flared into life and she applied it to the wick of the lamp she was holding, unaware that she was presenting him with an unrestricted view of her face, made golden in the soft light, golden and very beautiful. "Besides, I don't know yet that you're well enough for what I have in mind."

He looked smug. "I'm well enough."

She put the lamp down on the bedside table, standing back out of the circle of light. She had the advantage of him now and she stood there, waiting, loving him with her eyes.

"My father was ill for weeks with malaria," she remembered.

"They don't allow you to be ill with anything these days," he assured her comfortably. "Either you get better, or you die of it, but malingering has gone out of fashion."

"You shouldn't have given me your tablet."

He reached out for her and caught her by the

wrist, pulling her down beside him. "My dear girl,
it's time you knew I'd rather suffer a thousand
hells myself than see you suffer a bad moment—"

"You sent me away!"

"Only because I thought I couldn't have you."

"You should have told me about Tumi. What
else was I to think? How was I to know she wasn't
your mistress?"

"You never asked."

"I was jealous."

"And I was noble and stupid."

"Yes, you were," she agreed. She relaxed
against his shoulder, pulling his arms more closely
about her. "You could have made me listen."

"I was hoping you loved me enough to trust me
to do the right thing by you. If Tumi had been my
mistress you never would have known a thing
about her. Didn't you know that?"

"No," she said honestly, "I didn't. I'd never
been jealous before, and it isn't the kind of
emotion that allows much scope for objective
thought. There was something else, too, that
made me think—" She took a deep breath.
"You're not going to like this!" she warned him.

"I suppose it has to do with Timothy?" he said
dryly. "You think I'm like Timothy?"

She shook her head until her hair flew. "When
I'd calmed down a bit, I knew I'd been a worse
fool than you were, but by that time you'd told
me to go."

"Another rejection you had to learn to live
with?"

She was shocked that he'd read her so well. "I
should have known better," she acknowledged.

She ran the palm of her hand over his chest with a new-born pride of possession. "However, I'm not going to apologise again, Joel Buchanan. You should have known better too! What's your excuse?"

He rewarded her with a lop-sided smile. "Would you believe jealousy? I've only had to think of you and Timothy together to see red for years now. You were mine, not his!"

"Mmm, so Rosamund kept hinting. But, surely, once you knew what our marriage had been like—"

"You still bear his name. I shan't be sure of you, my love, until you're Mrs. Joel Buchanan!"

She was hard put to it not to laugh. "In fact as well as in name?" she teased him, sounding more complacent than she meant to.

"Right!"

Her mood changed as she considered all that the change in name implied.

"I didn't know you wanted to *marry* me," she began cautiously. "You never mentioned it before." She stirred restlessly, still savouring the changes in her life that having Joel as her husband would bring. "Are you sure? I mean, have you thought it all out? There was an awful lot of gossip about me and Timothy, some of it very ugly, some of it absolutely unbearable. It would be bound to rear its ugly head again if we got married. Joel, you don't know what it was like!" Her voice quavered dangerously. "There was nobody on my side—not even Timothy."

She was flat on her back and he was leaning over her with an expression so stern that she couldn't breathe properly. The pulse at her throat throbbed violently until she wondered if it were panic or something much sweeter that was seizing up her senses.

"Joel?"

He blinked, his long eye-lashes casting a fringe of shadow down his cheeks. She wished she could read his expression better, though there was no doubting the firmness with which his arms surrounded her, hugging her close up against the hardness of his lithe, muscular body.

"I was on your side," he said in an angry burst. "I was always on your side, only you wouldn't forget even for a moment that you were Timothy Gregson's wife! If I'd known you'd split up, I'd have carried you off by force if need be. I kept asking where you were and what you were doing, but nobody seemed to know. I badgered your mother to death, until I had to believe she didn't know where you were and that you didn't write to her—"

"They didn't want to know! I felt like a traitor to them, and Timothy knew I was a traitor to him, too, in my heart, but I was married to him, like it or not, and I determined to stick by him as long as he wanted me to. When he didn't want me around, I could hardly go back to my parents and say, 'Well, here am I, back again,' could I? I'd hurt them too badly for that!"

"You could have come to me!"

"Because you'd seen me one day in Nairobi and wanted to go to bed with me? For all I knew you were married and ecstatically happy with someone else!"

His mouth jerked. "You should have known better than that, my beautiful Pippa. There's been no one else since that day. At first it made me burning mad that a wee slip of a girl in a badly fitting dress could have such an effect on me. There was even a time when I wanted to hurt you as much as you were hurting me! But when I saw you again, all I wanted was to take you into my arms and love you, just as I had before, and now you were *available!* You were mine for the taking, even if you had been Timothy's first, but you didn't seem to recognise what we were going to mean to each other."

Pippa opened her eyes wide. "Is that how it seemed to you? I was devastated by your appearance at my father's camp. I thought it must have been written all over me! But I was embarrassed too. You have to admit I was in an awkward predicament. I hardly expected you to be *pleased* that Timothy thought so little of me as a woman that he'd never taken me to bed with him."

Joel grinned at her, his eyes alight with an emotion that made her tremble. "Kiss me, Pippa!" he commanded her.

She put her mouth against his, exploring his lips with the tip of her tongue. It was the end of her freedom of action. With a groan, his arms came up around her, and he reversed their positions until she could feel his whole weight resting on her lower body, trapping her tightly against him.

"Never go away from me again!" he murmured harshly. "I love you, Pippa. I need you beside me always!"

His kiss hurt her mouth but she didn't care. She

arched her back to welcome him closer still, mildly surprised to find he was stark naked under the sheet. What was more, he seemed to want her to be in a similar condition, for he had already disposed of her shirt, his hands delighting in the soft curves of her breasts. She thought she would explode with joy as he caressed her nipples, his breathing deepening to match her own.

A door slammed down below. Joel rolled away from her, groaning.

"We've had the goats, and people who should have known better, who can it be now?"

"They won't come up here," Pippa said with more confidence than she felt.

Joel listened for a moment. "Want to bet?" he asked grimly. He searched the floor with one hand, finding her shirt and handing it to her. At the same moment the telephone bell shrilled beside the bed.

"Don't answer it!" Pippa suggested, not even trying to put on her shirt.

But he already had. "What d'you want?" he demanded of the unseen caller. "Yes she is. Yes we are. No, don't come! We'll come to Nairobi and visit you when we're good and ready, certainly not for a week or so. No, you can't speak to her! I'll tell her you send your love." He slammed the receiver back into its socket.

"Rosamund?" Pippa hazarded.

"She wants to come to the wedding."

"What wedding?"

The frustration fell away from him and he laughed. "Our wedding, my love. She's under the impression that she sent you running down here to marry me before I fell apart entirely. As sisters go, she's always been the most observant I've ever come across. Only she would have known how desperate I was after you took me at my word and left me standing. Why hadn't I told you about Tumi, she demanded. I felt a right fool when I had to admit that I'd wanted to make you as jealous as I'd been of that wretched husband of yours!"

Pippa stuck to the one salient point. "We're getting married?"

"How else are you going to become Mrs. Joel Buchanan?"

Pippa swallowed, trying to control her leaping senses. "I don't know. I hadn't thought . . . Oh, Joel, are you sure?"

He took both her hands in his, ensuring that he had her full attention. "My love, I'm not and never shall be anything like Timothy Gregson. I've every intention of loving you as often and as thoroughly as I can entice you to put up with me—"

"I'd stay with you anyway!" she burst out.

He shook his head, his hair like fire in the light from the lamp. "That might have suited me once, but now I think we both need the security of marriage, don't you? Marriage means commitment. Once the knot's tied it'll take you years to untie it, if you ever manage it, and I'll be doing my best to see that you don't—"

"*Me?* Why should I want to leave you?"

"You've walked away from me before now!"

Her throat felt dry and her tongue like a lump of wood in her mouth. "I was married to Timothy then. I didn't like it—in fact it nearly killed me—but I owed him my loyalty even if he didn't want it—or me! But with you, my darling, I want to share my whole life, not a duty I've been trapped into. I love you!"

"There must have been a time when you thought you loved Timothy!"

The pain in his voice made her heart contract. "It might have been different if I had loved him," she said quietly, "but I didn't. I thought he'd be someone of my own, someone who'd always be there, who'd be more interested in me than in his job, or whatever. I didn't love him, but I thought he loved me and that I could give him enough if I worked hard enough at it. It turned out he didn't love me either. He didn't love anybody. He was even less interested in me than everyone else had been and I can't blame him for that. It was all my own fault. I ruined both our lives."

Joel lifted her bodily into his arms, the discarded shirt falling once more to the floor. "I could say I want to marry you so that you'll never be lonely again, but I'm too selfish for that. I can't do without you, Pippa, as Rosamund will have told you. When you're not beside me I'm only half a man. Will you marry me and make me complete?"

She gave him her lips. "We'll complete each other," she promised.

"*Hodi!* Anyone there? I'm coming up!"

Pippa could feel Joel shaking with laughter. "What would we do without our relations?" he muttered.

She pulled away from him, snatching up her

shirt and battling her way into it, doing up the
buttons with fingers that flatly refused to follow
the urgent messages from her brain.

"We're not married yet!" she reminded him
tartly. "And it's my mother who's coming up the
stairs—at least yours do it by telephone!"

Mrs. Walker barely knocked on the door as she
came into the room. She glanced at her dishev-
elled daughter with evident surprise before she
turned to smile at Joel.

"I've finished here at last! I came to tell you
I'm going back to Malindi first thing in the morning—"

"You can't, Mother!" Pippa interrupted her.
"Joel and I are getting married—"

"You don't need me for that," Mrs. Walker
retorted dryly. "In fact I feel decidedly *de trop*
already."

"But you'll have to come to the ceremony!"
Pippa protested.

"Why? I'm not marrying Joel. If I were to take
time off every time you decided to get married—"

"You weren't there last time either!" Pippa
wailed.

"No," her mother agreed. "Then, I stayed
away in case I did or said something I would
regret."

"And what's your excuse this time?" Joel asked
her in tones as languid as her own.

"This time I'll be busy telling everyone the
good news," Mrs. Walker retorted with a twinkle.
"Rosamund and I are going to be frightfully busy
telling it our way before anyone else gets an
opportunity to look backwards instead of for-

wards. It'll be a frightful bore, especially just now, but you can consider it my wedding present to you both—or rather one of them. I brought you this as probably my first and last maternal gesture towards Pippa. Knowing her, and that prickly conscience of hers, she'll feel much more comfortable if you wait until after you've tied the knot, dear boy." She held out the piece of paper to Joel but her eyes were on her daughter's scarlet face. She shook her head slowly from side to side. "You'd better get married first thing in the morning if that's the way things are going. Meanwhile—"

"Joel might not be well enough in the morning. Malaria comes and goes."

"He was in and out of bed like a jack-in-the-box before you came running back to nurse him!"

Pippa turned wide eyes on Joel. "I suppose you did have malaria?" she accused him.

"I did have a temperature—"

"Malaria?"

"Bad temper," Mrs. Walker answered for him. "He thought he'd blown it. He was unbearable! Only Rosamund's promise to get you back down here stopped me from taking my leave also, I assure you!"

Pippa fell on Joel in pretended anger and was rewarded by a hard kiss that took her breath away. She took the piece of paper her mother had given him out of his hand to give herself time to recover and saw that it was a special licence, allowing them to get married anywhere in Kenya at a few hours' notice.

"Oh, Mother!" she exclaimed.

Mrs. Walker was already on her way out of the room. "Yes, well, even the most indifferent parents have their uses, dear," she said lightly over her shoulder. "That was just to show that this time you have my blessing and my good wishes for a very happy life together."

Pippa ran after her, catching up with her on the stairs and enveloping her in an enthusiastic hug. "Thanks," she said and, ignoring Mrs. Walker's half-hearted efforts to get away, hugged her all over again.

"Well, Mrs. Buchanan?"

Pippa stretched, smiling. "Very well indeed!" She held out her arms to him. "If I'd known what I know now, I would never have been able to resist you in Nairobi. I'm sorry I wasted so much time—" She broke off, her smile changing to a gasp as he took advantage of her lassitude to move in closer than she had expected.

"It's better this way," he answered her. "There's nothing to come between us now. If I had had you then, I never would have allowed you to go back to Timothy."

Pippa knew he was speaking the truth. She shivered inwardly as she thought of the revenge Timothy would have exacted from her.

"Don't think about it," Joel advised her. "There's nothing he can do to you now! I mean to love you until you can't remember what it was like before you came to live with me."

"I love you," she said aloud.

His eyes lit with a gleam that made her blush. "Good. Keep working at it and you won't hear any complaints from me. I hope you're not thinking of getting up for breakfast quite yet?"

"Certainly not," she agreed demurely.

It was a long time before Joel left her alone in the enormous bed she had shared with him on their wedding night. He had told her this was the bedroom he usually used when he was at home, rather than the harem quarters where she had found him brooding over her absence. It was a fine room of majestic proportions, but it told her very little else about him. There was little furniture to speak of apart from the bed, and there was nothing of his left lying about to betray his many interests. Only a blown-up photograph of a herd of elephants spoke of his work amongst the animals of East Africa, and she suspected that that was new. He might even have hung it there in her honour.

She heard the sound of the shower and rose reluctantly to join him. A breeze was blowing across the island, and it looked as if it were going to be a beautiful day.

"Getting hungry?" he asked her as she joined him under the primitive shower, as naked as he.

She shook her head, putting her hands up onto his shoulders and smoothing the water over his hard muscles.

"I just wanted to say thank you. I'm going to enjoy being Mrs. Joel Buchanan!"

He bent his head and claimed her lips, holding her close against him as the water pounded down on them both.

"Just remember that I love you, Pippa darling, that I always have and always will."

"I love you too," she responded, equally solemn.

His smile brought an answering bubble of mirth to her throat as he handed her the soap and his flannel. "One of the first duties of a wife is to scrub her husband's back—"

"Only if you're going to scrub mine!"

"It's a deal," he agreed.

He lifted her out of the shower and carried her back to the bed, drying her carefully with the top loose sheet.

"In an hour or so we'll have brunch, and then we'll go sailing, and then we'll come back here—"

Pippa began to laugh. "And then we'll make love again," she finished for him. "I couldn't have thought of a nicer programme myself."

Genuine Silhouette sterling silver bookmark for only $15.95!

What a beautiful way to hold your place in your current romance! This genuine sterling silver bookmark, with the distinctive Silhouette symbol in elegant black, measures 1½" long and 1" wide. It makes a beautiful gift for yourself, and for every romantic you know! And, at only $15.95 each, including all postage and handling charges, you'll want to order several now, while supplies last.

Send your name and address with check or money order for $15.95 per bookmark ordered to
Simon & Schuster Enterprises
120 Brighton Rd., P.O. Box 5020
Clifton, N.J. 07012
Attn: Bookmark

Bookmarks can be ordered pre-paid only. No charges will be accepted. Please allow 4-6 weeks for delivery.

N.Y. State Residents
Please Add Sales Tax

Silhouette Romance

IT'S YOUR OWN SPECIAL TIME

Contemporary romances for today's women.
Each month, six very special love stories will be yours
from SILHOUETTE.

$1.75 each

☐ 100 Stanford	☐ 127 Roberts	☐ 155 Hampson	☐ 182 Clay
☐ 101 Hardy	☐ 128 Hampson	☐ 156 Sawyer	☐ 183 Stanley
☐ 102 Hastings	☐ 129 Converse	☐ 157 Vitek	☐ 184 Hardy
☐ 103 Cork	☐ 130 Hardy	☐ 158 Reynolds	☐ 185 Hampson
☐ 104 Vitek	☐ 131 Stanford	☐ 159 Tracy	☐ 186 Howard
☐ 105 Eden	☐ 132 Wisdom	☐ 160 Hampson	☐ 187 Scott
☐ 106 Dailey	☐ 133 Rowe	☐ 161 Trent	☐ 188 Cork
☐ 107 Bright	☐ 134 Charles	☐ 162 Ashby	☐ 189 Stephens
☐ 108 Hampson	☐ 135 Logan	☐ 163 Roberts	☐ 190 Hampson
☐ 109 Vernon	☐ 136 Hampson	☐ 164 Browning	☐ 191 Browning
☐ 110 Trent	☐ 137 Hunter	☐ 165 Young	☐ 192 John
☐ 111 South	☐ 138 Wilson	☐ 166 Wisdom	☐ 193 Trent
☐ 112 Stanford	☐ 139 Vitek	☐ 167 Hunter	☐ 194 Barry
☐ 113 Browning	☐ 140 Erskine	☐ 168 Carr	☐ 195 Dailey
☐ 114 Michaels	☐ 142 Browning	☐ 169 Scott	☐ 196 Hampson
☐ 115 John	☐ 143 Roberts	☐ 170 Ripy	☐ 197 Summers
☐ 116 Lindley	☐ 144 Goforth	☐ 171 Hill	☐ 198 Hunter
☐ 117 Scott	☐ 145 Hope	☐ 172 Browning	☐ 199 Roberts
☐ 118 Dailey	☐ 146 Michaels	☐ 173 Camp	☐ 200 Lloyd
☐ 119 Hampson	☐ 147 Hampson	☐ 174 Sinclair	☐ 201 Starr
☐ 120 Carroll	☐ 148 Cork	☐ 175 Jarrett	☐ 202 Hampson
☐ 121 Langan	☐ 149 Saunders	☐ 176 Vitek	☐ 203 Browning
☐ 122 Scofield	☐ 150 Major	☐ 177 Dailey	☐ 204 Carroll
☐ 123 Sinclair	☐ 151 Hampson	☐ 178 Hampson	☐ 205 Maxam
☐ 124 Beckman	☐ 152 Halston	☐ 179 Beckman	☐ 206 Manning
☐ 125 Bright	☐ 153 Dailey	☐ 180 Roberts	☐ 207 Windham
☐ 126 St. George	☐ 154 Beckman	☐ 181 Terrill	

$1.95 each

☐ 208 Halston	☐ 212 Young	☐ 216 Saunders	☐ 220 Hampson
☐ 209 LaDame	☐ 213 Dailey	☐ 217 Vitek	☐ 221 Browning
☐ 210 Eden	☐ 214 Hampson	☐ 218 Hunter	☐ 222 Carroll
☐ 211 Walters	☐ 215 Roberts	☐ 219 Cork	☐ 223 Summers

Silhouette Romance

IT'S YOUR OWN SPECIAL TIME
Contemporary romances for today's women.
Each month, six very special love stories will be yours
from SILHOUETTE. Look for them wherever books are sold
or order now from the coupon below.

$1.95 each

☐ 224 Langan	☐ 241 Wisdom	☐ 258 Ashby	☐ 275 Browning
☐ 225 St. George	☐ 242 Brooke	☐ 259 English	☐ 276 Vernon
☐ 226 Hamson	☐ 243 Saunders	☐ 260 Martin	☐ 277 Wilson
☐ 227 Beckman	☐ 244 Sinclair	☐ 261 Saunders	☐ 278 Hunter
☐ 228 King	☐ 245 Trent	☐ 262 John	☐ 279 Ashby
☐ 229 Thornton	☐ 246 Carroll	☐ 263 Wilson	☐ 280 Roberts
☐ 230 Stevens	☐ 247 Halldorson	☐ 264 Vine	☐ 281 Lovan
☐ 231 Dailey	☐ 248 St. George	☐ 265 Adams	☐ 282 Halldorson
☐ 232 Hampson	☐ 249 Scofield	☐ 266 Trent	☐ 283 Payne
☐ 233 Vernon	☐ 250 Hampson	☐ 267 Chase	☐ 284 Young
☐ 234 Smith	☐ 251 Wilson	☐ 268 Hunter	☐ 285 Gray
☐ 235 James	☐ 252 Roberts	☐ 269 Smith	☐ 286 Cork
☐ 236 Maxam	☐ 253 James	☐ 270 Camp	☐ 287 Joyce
☐ 237 Wilson	☐ 254 Palmer	☐ 271 Allison	☐ 288 Smith
☐ 238 Cork	☐ 255 Smith	☐ 272 Forrest	☐ 289 Saunders
☐ 239 McKay	☐ 256 Hampson	☐ 273 Beckman	☐ 290 Hunter
☐ 240 Hunter	☐ 257 Hunter	☐ 274 Roberts	☐ 291 McKay

SILHOUETTE BOOKS, Department SB/1
1230 Avenue of the Americas
New York, NY 10020

Please send me the books I have checked above. I am enclosing $_____
(please add 75¢ to cover postage and handling. NYS and NYC residents please
add appropriate sales tax). Send check or money order—no cash or C.O.D.'s
please. Allow six weeks for delivery.

NAME _____

ADDRESS _____

CITY _____ STATE/ZIP _____

Coming Next Month

Journey To Quiet Waters by Dixie Browning

Ivy had regretted the sale of her family estate. And now
Hunter Smith, the new owner, arrogantly demanded the use
of the house *and* her services—and soon captured
her heart as well.

Behind Closed Doors by Diana Morgan

Troubleshooter Spencer McIntyre had been called in to
untangle the mess Emily Moreau had playfully programmed
into the company computer. Now the computer seemed
determined to get the battling couple together.

Beloved Pirate by Ann Cockcroft

Laura knew that famous author Jared Tanner had earned his
reputation as an unscrupulous lover. But on the romantic
Spanish island of Mallorca, common sense—and her fiance
back home—seemed very far away.

That Tender Feeling by Dorothy Vernon

Ros Seymour was a top-notch chef but somehow she couldn't
seem to do anything right when devastating Cliff Heath was
around. It seemed she'd need more than her culinary skills to
convince him they were meant to be together.

South Of The Sun by Laurie Paige

It was a physical challenge to be the only woman on an
expedition to the desolate wilderness of the South Pole, but
Jordie soon found a greater challenge in resisting the
impossibly attractive scientist Jarl Ericson.

A Separate Happiness by Brittany Young

Brianna knew that Caesare De Alvarado was playing a
dangerous and deadly game to help his people. Their love
could be fatal, but try as she might, Brianna
couldn't stay away.